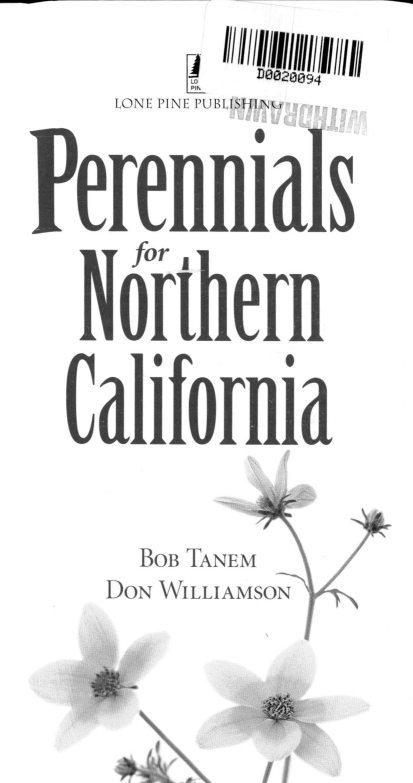

LONE PINE PUBLISHING

Perennials
for Northern California

BOB TANEM
DON WILLIAMSON

D0020094

The Publisher: Lone Pine Publishing

10145 – 81 Avenue	1901 Raymond Ave. SW, Suite C
Edmonton, AB T6E 1W9	Renton, WA 98055
Canada	USA

Website: http://www.lonepinepublishing.com

Canadian Cataloguing in Publication Data

Tanem, Bob, 1930–
   Perennials for northern California
   Includes index.
   ISBN 1-55105-251-2

   1. Perennials—California. 2. Gardening—California. I. Williamson, Don, 1962– II. Title.
SB434.T36 2002   635.9'32'09794   C2001-911421-4

Editorial Director: Nancy Foulds
Project Editor: Shelagh Kubish
Editorial: Shelagh Kubish, Dawn Loewen, Denise Dykstra
Illustrations Coordinator: Carol Woo
Photo Editor: Don Williamson
Production Project Coordinator: Heather Markham
Book Design: Heather Markham
Cover Design: Robert Weidemann, Rod Michalchuk
Layout & Production: Heather Markham, Tina Tomljenovic
Image Editing: Elliot Engley, Jeff Fedorkiw, Tina Tomljenovic, Arlana Anderson-Hale
Scanning, Separations & Film: Elite Lithographers Co. Ltd.

Photography: All photographs by Tim Matheson or Tamara Eder except Karen Carriere 125b, 153a & c, 155a & b, 221a, b & c; Joan de Grey 212, 213a; Therese D'Monte 74, 75b, 165a, 275b, 279b; Elliot Engley 48a, b, c & d; Anne Gordon 199b; Al Harvey 191a; Horticultural Photography 121b, 213b, 269b; Horticultural Photography/Maleah Taubman 311a; Horticultural Photography/Marilyn Warford 218, 311b; Janet Loughrey 119a, 148b, 159b, 180, 226a, 249b, 267a, 287b & c, 335b; Erika Markham 53a & b; David McDonald 44, 123, 191b, 227b, 264a, 280b; Kim Patrick O'Leary 13, 14a, 17b, 22a, 24b, 27a & b, 39a, 49a, 50b, 54b, 56a & b, 57b, 59a, 63a, 69, 97a, 125a, 150, 151, 161a & b, 175a & b, 185a, 199a, 210, 211a & b, 234, 235a & b, 236a & b, 237, 246, 247a & b, 248, 249a, 286, 287a, 290b, 306, 307, 308a & b, 309a & b, 323a; Joy Spurr 12, 14b, 16c, 23c, 117a, 335a; Peter Thompstone 91b, 117b, 171b, 172a, 185b, 189b, 193a, 202a, 203a, 205b, 226b, 266, 268a & b, 269a, 280a, 302, 303a, 315c; Valleybrook Gardens 122, 219b, 220, 263b, 264b, 310.

Front cover photographs (clockwise from top left) by Tim Matheson, bleeding heart, bellflower, Shasta daisy, cranesbill, daylily; *by Therese D'Monte,* aster

Zones map: Elliot Engley, Ian Dawe; based on USDA hardiness zones map

We acknowledge the financial support of the Government of Canada through the Book Publishing Industry Development Program (BPIDP) for our publishing activities.

PC: P4

Contents

Acknowledgments

WE GRATEFULLY ACKNOWLEDGE THE FOLLOWING NURSERIES FOR their cooperation: West End Nursery in San Rafael, Sunnyside Nursery in San Anselmo, Sloat Garden Center in Novato and BaySide Gardens in Belvedere. Lee and Mary Grace Bertsch allowed photographs to be taken in their garden. We thank the staff at Fioli, Elizabeth Gamble Gardens, Bonfante Gardens in Gilroy, the Leininger Community Center, Strybing Arboretum and Botanical Garden and the VanDusen Botanical Garden in Victoria, B.C. Thanks also to Kawahara Wholesale Nursery, Gaddis Nursery and Emerisa Gardens for furnishing their current plant availability lists.

The authors wish to thank Alison Beck, author of several Lone Pine gardening books, for her contributions to the text.

Bob Tanem would like to thank his customer base of 40 years, the radio station personnel and Kit Lynch, who encouraged the station to put his garden show on the air. He also thanks his wife, Bev, for her patience and sacrifices of time spent alone while he was working on this project. Most of all, he thanks the Good Lord for allowing him to retain his memory after 71 years.

Don Williamson extends thanks to his mother, Margaret Williamson, and his late father, John Williamson, for their love and support. He also thanks the team at Lone Pine Publishing, without whose help none of this would be possible. Don would also like to thank The Creator.

The Perennials at a Glance

PICTORIAL GUIDE IN ALPHABETICAL ORDER, BY COMMON NAME

Anemone
p. 70

Aster
p. 74

Astilbe
p. 78

Baby's Breath
p. 82

Balloon Flower
p. 86

Basket-of-Gold
p. 88

Bear's Breeches
p. 90

Beard Tongue
p. 94

Bee Balm
p. 98

Bellflower
p. 102

Bergenia
p. 106

Bidens
p. 110

Black-eyed Susan
p. 112

Blue Eyes
p. 118

Blue Star Flower
p. 122

Bleeding Heart
p. 114

Blue Marguerite
p. 120

Butterfly Weed
p. 124

California Poppy
p. 126

Candle Larkspur
p. 130

Candytuft
p. 134

Cape Fuchsia
p. 136

Cardinal Flower
p. 138

Catmint
p. 142

Columbine
p. 146

Copper Canyon Daisy
p. 150

Coral Bells
p. 152

Coreopsis
p. 156

Cranesbill
p. 160

Dame's Rocket
p. 164

Daylily
p. 166

Dianthus
p. 170

Dusty Miller
p. 174

Euphorbia
p. 176

Evening Primrose
p. 180

False Rockcress
p. 182

Fan Flower
p. 184

Fleabane
p. 186

Foamflower
p. 188

Foxglove
p. 190

Gaura
p. 194

Gayfeather
p. 196

Geranium
p. 198

Geum
p. 204

Gunnera
p. 210

Hellebore
p. 212

Globe Thistle
p. 206

Golden Marguerite
p. 208

Hens and Chicks
p. 214

Himalayan Poppy
p. 222

Iris
p. 224

Hibiscus
p. 218

Lady's Mantle
p. 230

Lamb's Ears
p. 232

Jacob's Ladder
p. 228

Lavender Cotton
p. 238

Ligularia
p. 240

Lantana
p. 234

Lion's Tail
p. 246

Lithodora
p. 248

Lily-of-the-Nile
p. 242

Lungwort
p. 256

Lupine
p. 252

Mallow
p. 256

Marsh Marigold
p. 260

Meadow Rue
p. 262

Meadowsweet
p. 266

Monkey Flower
p. 270

Monkshood
p. 272

Obedient Plant
p. 276

Oriental Poppy
p. 278

Peruvian Lily
p. 286

Phlox
p. 288

Peony
p. 282

Plantain Lily
p. 294

Purple Coneflower
p. 298

Pincushion Flower
p. 292

Rock Cress
p. 302

Russian Sage
p. 304

Salvia
p. 306

Sandwort
p. 310

Shasta Daisy
p. 316

Soapwort
p. 318

Sea Holly
p. 312

Sea Pink
p. 314

Stokes' Aster
p. 320

Stonecrop
p. 322

Sweet Woodruff
p. 326

Thyme
p. 328

Torch Lily
p. 332

Violet
p. 334

Wallflower
p. 336

Yarrow
p. 338

To Sheri
With fondest
regards Jan em
Bob

Introduction

PERENNIALS ARE PLANTS THAT TAKE THREE OR MORE YEARS TO complete their life cycle. This is a broad definition that includes trees and shrubs. To narrow the definition in the garden we refer to herbaceous (non-woody) perennials as perennials. Herbaceous perennials live for three or more years, but they generally die back to the ground at the end of the growing season and start fresh with new shoots each spring. Some plants grouped with perennials do not die back completely—for example subshrubs such as thyme. Still others—evergreen perennials such as dianthus, Lamb's Ears and some daylilies—remain green all winter.

Though the climate of all of Northern California is considered temperate, there is a great deal of diversity within this area. In coastal regions the summer temperatures are usually 65 to 80° F during the day, cooling to 55 to 60° F overnight. There are usually two or three heat spikes to around 100° F in June and again in September. Summer temperatures in the interior valleys are usually 80–100° F from mid-June through August, cooling to 70° F at night. Humidity in the state is not usually a problem except where summer fog persists daily. Another humid area would be the northern part of the Central Valley where rice is the main crop grown.

Winter conditions vary widely across Northern California. In general, Northern California winters in the interior valleys have fairly consistent rain. The temperatures in the interior valleys are cold enough to provide ample dormancy for perennials to set flowers for the following summer. However, the moderate climate of coastal regions does not.

No matter how challenging the site, there are perennials that will flourish and provide the gardener with an almost limitless selection of colors, sizes and forms. This versatility, along with the beauty and permanence of perennials, lies at the root of the continued and growing popularity of perennials.

There is more to consider when growing perennials in Northern California than climate. The great diversity in soil types and growing conditions is a lesson in the varied geology of the state. The coastal areas of the west and its mountain chain will dictate many kinds of gardens where you can grow just about anything. The soil itself may consist of clay or sand and is mostly alkaline. In contrast, gardeners living in the interior valleys will deal with alluvial soils rich in nutrients and a neutral to slightly acidic pH. Marked all over with fertile river valleys and floodplains, Northern California provides one of the most interesting, challenging and rewarding places to create a perennial garden.

Don't feel too limited by information on large-scale climate zones, perennial hardiness and soil patterns. Microclimates abound. The proximity of buildings, how quickly the soil drains and whether you garden in a low, cold hollow or on top of a wind-swept knoll or hillside affect the microclimate of your own garden. The challenge of gardening with plants that are borderline hardy is part of the fun of growing perennials.

Plants listed in this book as **hardy** will grow anywhere in Northern California.

Semi-hardy perennials will survive with some mulching or protection with a row cover if temperatures drop below 32° F. The plants classified in this book as **semi-hardy** will survive in zones 9a to 9b, even with minimal winter protection.

Tender perennials are very frost sensitive and will usually die when temperatures dip below 32° F. The perennials classified in this book as

Average Annual Mimimum Temperature

Zone	Temp (°F)
4b	-20 to -25
5a	-15 to -20
5b	-10 to -15
6a	-5 to -10
6b	0 to -5
7a	5 to 0
7b	10 to 5
8a	15 to 10
8b	20 to 15
9a	25 to 20
9b	30 to 25
10a	35 to 30

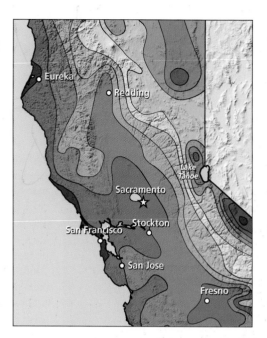

tender can be expected to survive in zone 10a. Using mulch will protect tender perennials from freeze and thaw cycles in winter. A 2–3" layer of organic mulch, such as shredded cedar bark, will provide adequate protection. Cedar bark has the added bonus of having some anti-fungal properties.

Many enthusiastic and creative people, both amateur and professional, are involved in gardening in the state. Individual growers, breeders, societies, schools, publications and public gardens provide information, encouragement and fruitful debate for the gardener. California gardeners nurture a knowledge of planting and propagation methods and a plethora of opinions on what is best for any patch of ground. Outstanding garden shows, county fairs, public gardens, arboretums and

private gardens in all of California attract literally crowds of people almost all year long. These events and locations are sources of inspiration as well as information. Perennials are relatively inexpensive and easy to share with friends and neighbors, which leads to more variety and wonderful discoveries. There are tropical enthusiasts that have added many varieties to the palette of choices for Northern California perennial gardens. The more varieties you try, the more likely you'll be to discover what loves to grow in your garden. It allows you to experience successes that you probably otherwise would not have encountered. Our advice: 'Dig in and grow for it.'

Perennial Gardens

PERENNIALS CAN BE USED ALONE in a garden or combined with other plants. Perennials form a bridge in the garden between the permanent structure provided by trees and shrubs and the temporary color provided by annuals. They often flower longer and grow to mature size more quickly than shrubs do and in many cases require less care and are less prone to pests and diseases than annuals are.

Perennials can be included in any type, size or style of garden. From the riot of color in a cottage garden or the cool, soothing shades of green in a woodland garden to a welcoming cluster of pots on a doorstep, perennials open up a world of design possibilities for even the inexperienced gardener.

Variegated Obedient Plant (above), Gaura (center)

It is very important when planning your garden to decide what you like. If you enjoy the plants that are in your garden, then you are more likely to take proper care of them. Decide what style of garden you like as well as what plants you like. Think about the gardens you have most admired in your neighborhood, in books or while visiting friends. Use these ideas as starting points for planning your own garden.

A good perennial garden can be interesting throughout the year. Consider the foliage of the perennials you want to use. Foliage can be bold or flimsy, coarse or refined; it can be big or small, light or dark; its color can vary from yellow, grey, blue or purple to any multitude of greens; and it can be striped, splashed, edged, dotted or mottled. The texture can be shiny, fuzzy, silky, rough or smooth. The famous white gardens at Sissinghurst, England,

Fine-textured Astilbe (left & background), with coarse-textured Plaintain Lily (foreground)

were designed not to showcase a haphazard collection of white flowers but to remove the distraction of color and allow the eye to linger on the foliage to appreciate its subtle appeal. Flowers come and go, but a garden planned with careful attention to foliage will always be interesting.

Select perennials that flower at different times in order to have some part of your garden flowering all season. (See Quick Reference Chart, p. 342.)

Next, consider the size and shape of different perennials. Choose a variety of forms to make your garden more interesting. The size of your garden influences these decisions, but do not limit a small garden to small perennials or a large garden to large perennials. Use a balanced combination of plant sizes that are in scale with their specific location. (See Quick Reference Chart, p. 342.)

Daylily (above) and Mexican Sage (below) are low-maintenance perennials.

Hibiscus (above), Ligularia (center)

Bleeding Heart (below)

There are many colors of perennials. Not only do flower colors vary, but foliage colors vary as well. Different colors have different effects on our senses. Cool colors, such as blue, purple and green, are soothing and make small spaces seem bigger. Warm colors, such as red, orange and yellow, are more stimulating and appear to fill large spaces. (See Quick Reference Chart, p. 342.)

Textures can also create a sense of space; some gardens are designed solely by texture. Larger leaves are considered coarse in texture and the fact that they are visible from a greater distance make spaces seem smaller and more shaded. Small leaves, or those that are finely divided, are considered fine in texture and create a sense of greater space and light.

Coarse-textured Perennials

Bear's Breeches
Bergenia
Black-eyed Susan
Gunnera
Hibiscus
Lamb's Ears
Ligularia
Lungwort
Meadowsweet
Plantain Lily
Purple Coneflower
Sedum 'Autumn Joy'
Torch Lily

Fine-textured Perennials
Astilbe
Baby's Breath
Bleeding Heart
Columbine
Coreopsis
Cranesbill
Fleabane
Gaura
Lavender Cotton
Meadow Rue
Thyme
Yarrow

Lavender Cotton (above), Pincushion Flower (center)

Decide how much time you will have to devote to your garden. With good planning and preparation, you can enjoy low-maintenance perennial gardens. Consider using plants that perform well with little maintenance and ones that are generally pest- and disease-free.

Low-maintenance Perennials
Aster
Bee Balm*
Black-eyed Susan
California Poppy
Cleveland Sage
Coral Bells
Coreopsis
Daylily
Dianthus
Euphorbia
Mexican Sage
Pincushion Flower
Plantain Lily
Russian Sage
Shasta Daisy
(*may take over garden)

Torch Lily (below)

Getting Started

ONCE YOU HAVE SOME IDEAS about what you want in your garden, consider the growing conditions. Plants growing in ideal conditions—or conditions as close to ideal as you can get them—are healthier and less prone to pest and disease problems than plants growing in stressful conditions. Some plants considered high maintenance become low maintenance when grown in the right conditions.

If you are not sure of the textures or colors of certain plants and flowers, a visit to a local nursery to see the plants growing will be time well spent. Local nurseries can be a great help as you plan a perennial garden. Most nurseries have California Certified Professionals available to assist you. These are people who have passed the stringent tests of the California Association of Nurserymen. It is helpful to them if you bring a sketch of the area you intend to plant and include information as to the area's exposure to sun, shade and wind so that the nursery workers can help you choose plants for the area. There is no charge for this. Plus, if you take our book to the nursery with you, you will have information about the plants and pictures of them as well as the actual living, growing plants right there in front of you. Taking advantage of the help at the nurseries will go a long way to make your garden a dream come true.

Do not attempt to make your garden match the growing conditions of the plants you like. Instead, choose plants to match your garden conditions. The levels of light, the type of soil and the amount of exposure in your garden provide guidelines that make plant selection easier. A sketch of your garden, drawn on graph paper, may help you organize the various considerations as you plan. Knowing your growing conditions can prevent costly mistakes—plan ahead rather than correct later.

Light

There are four categories of light in a garden: full sun, partial shade, light shade and full shade. Available light is affected by buildings, trees, fences and the position of the sun at different times of the day and year. Knowing what light is available in your garden will help you determine where to place each plant.

Shade border (above), sunny border (below)

Plants in full-sun locations, such as along south-facing walls, receive direct sunlight for all or most of the day. Locations classified as partial sun or partial shade, such as east- or west-facing walls, receive direct sunlight for part of the day and shade for the rest. Light-shade locations receive shade for most or all of the day, although some sunlight does filter through to ground level. An example of a light-shade location might be the ground under a small-leaved tree such as a birch. Full-shade locations, which would include the north side of a house, receive no direct sunlight.

Lion's Tail (above), Evening Primrose (center)

A traditional herb bed (below) uses brick to hold in heat.

It is important to remember that the intensity of the full sun can vary. For example, heat can become trapped and magnified between buildings in a city, baking all but the most heat-tolerant plants there in a concrete oven. Conversely, the sheltered hollow in the shade that protects your heat-hating plants in the humid summer heat may become a frost trap in winter, killing tender plants that should otherwise survive.

Perennials for Full Sun

Basket-of-gold
California Poppy
Candytuft
Cleveland Sage
Coreopsis
Daylily
Euphorbia
Lion's Tail
Mallow
Mexican Sage
Phlox
Pincushion Flower
Russian Sage
Stonecrop
Thyme
Wallflower
Yarrow

Perennials for Full Shade

Astilbe
Bleeding Heart
Hellebore
Jacob's Ladder
Ligularia
Lungwort
Monkshood
Plantain Lily
Sweet Woodruff
Violet

Soil

Plants and the soil they grow in have a unique relationship. Many plant functions go on underground. Soil holds air, water, nutrients and organic matter. Plant roots depend upon these resources while using the soil to hold themselves upright.

Soil is made up of particles of different sizes. Sand particles are the largest. Water drains quickly out of sandy soil and quickly washes nutrients away. Sand has lots of air space and doesn't compact easily. Clay particles are the smallest and can be seen only through a microscope. Water penetrates clay very slowly and drains very slowly. Clay holds the most nutrients, but there is very little room for air, and clay compacts quite easily. Most soil is made up of a combination of different particle sizes. These soils are called loams.

Monkey Flower (above), Euphorbia (below)

Dry, exposed garden (below)

Russian Sage (above), Cranesbill (center)

Yarrow in a mixed border (below)

Perennials for Sandy Soil

Basket-of-gold
Cardinal Flower
Euphorbia
Evening Primrose
Lavender Cotton
Monkey Flower
Peruvian Lily
Russian Sage
Salvia
Stokes' Aster
Thyme

Perennials for Clay Soil

Black-eyed Susan
Blue Marguerite
Coreopsis
Cranesbill
Stonecrop
Torch Lily
Wallflower
Yarrow

The other aspect of soil to consider is the pH—the scale on which acidity or alkalinity is measured. Soil acidity or alkalinity influences which nutrients are available for plants. Most plants prefer a soil pH between 5.5 and 7.5. You can test your soil if you plan to amend it; testing kits are available at many nurseries and garden centers. Soil can be made more alkaline by adding horticultural lime. Soil can be made more acidic by adding peat moss, pine needles, alfalfa pellets or chopped oak leaves. Altering the pH of your soil takes a long time, often many years, and is not easy. If you are trying to grow only one or two plants that require a soil with a different pH from your existing soil, consider growing them in a container or raised bed where it will be easier to amend the pH as needed.

Another thing to consider is how quickly the water drains out of your soil. Rocky soil on a hillside will probably drain very quickly; plants that prefer a very well-drained soil could do well there. Low-lying areas tend to retain water longer and some areas may rarely drain at all. Moist areas can be used for plants that require a consistent water supply, and areas that stay wet can be used for plants that prefer boggy conditions.

Drainage can be improved in very wet areas by adding sand or gravel to the soil, by installing some form of drainage tile or by building raised beds. Use caution when adding sand to clay soils. Adding sand to clay can easily make your soil as hard as concrete. Consulting with nursery professionals before adding sand to your garden's heavy soil can prevent potential problems. One of the traps we can fall into is the belief that hillsides are always well drained. In Northern California, many hillsides are clay and although they are difficult to get wet during summer, the winter rains may saturate them. It is a good idea to remove any berms or other water retention devices around the plants during winter. These will have to be replaced during the summer. Water retention in sandy soil can be improved through the addition of organic matter.

Irises (above), Marsh Marigold (below)

Sea Holly (above), Globe Thistle (center)

Stokes' Aster in a mixed bed (below)

Perennials for Moist Soil
Astilbe
Bleeding Heart
Coral Bells
Gunnera
Hibiscus
Iris
Lady's Mantle
Ligularia
Lobelia
Lungwort
Marsh Marigold
Meadowsweet
Monkshood
Plantain Lily

Perennials for Dry Soil
Basket-of-gold
Butterfly Weed
Coreopsis
Euphorbia
Evening Primrose
False Rockcress
Lamb's Ears
Lion's Tail
Lupine
Pincushion Flower
Russian Sage
Sea Holly
Sea Pink
Stonecrop
Stokes' Aster
Yarrow

Exposure
Finally, consider the exposure in your garden. Wind, heat, cold and rain are some of the elements your garden is exposed to, and different plants are better adapted than others to withstand the potential damage of these forces. Buildings, walls, fences, hills, hedges and trees influence your

garden's exposure. Another consideration along the coastal climates is salt spray. Many perennials will tolerate salt spray, whether the location is along the coast or adjacent to the bay.

Perennials that Tolerate Salt Spray

Blue Marguerite
California Poppy
Catmint
Dusty Miller
Fleabane
Geranium
Geum
Globe Thistle
Hens and Chicks
Lamb's Ears
Lily-of-the-Nile
Sea Holly
Torch Lily

Wind in particular can cause extensive damage to your plants. Plants can become dehydrated in windy locations because they may not be able to draw water out of the soil fast enough to replace the water that is lost through the leaves. Tall, stiff-stemmed perennials can be knocked over or broken by strong winds. Some plants that do not require staking in a sheltered location may need to be staked in a more exposed one. Use plants that are recommended for exposed locations, or temper the effect of the wind with a hedge or some trees. A solid wall will create wind turbulence on the leeward side, while a looser structure, such as a hedge, breaks up the force of the wind and protects a larger area.

Perennials for Exposed Locations

Basket-of-gold
Beard Tongue
Black-eyed Susan
Candytuft
Columbine
Creeping Phlox
Euphorbia
Fleabane
Gaura
Globe Thistle
Lantana
Stonecrop (groundcover species)
Thyme
Torch Lily
Yarrow

Dusty Miller (above), Lantana (below)

Preparing the Garden

TAKING THE TIME TO PROPERLY prepare your flowerbeds before you plant will save you time and effort later. Many gardening problems can be avoided with good preparation and maintenance. Starting with as few weeds as possible and with well-prepared soil that has had organic material added will give your plants a good start.

Loosen the soil with a large garden fork and remove the weeds. Avoid working the soil when it is very wet or very dry because you will damage the soil structure by breaking down the pockets that hold air and water. Add organic matter and work it into the soil with a spade, fork or Rototiller.

Organic matter is an important component of soil. It increases the water-holding and nutrient-holding capacity of sandy soil and binds together the large particles. In a clay soil, organic matter increases the water-absorbing and draining potential by opening up spaces between the tiny particles. Common organic additives for your soil are grass clippings, shredded leaves, peat moss, chopped straw, well-rotted manure, alfalfa pellets and compost. Alfalfa pellets supply a range of nutrients including trace elements. They also contain a plant growth hormone. Bob uses alfalfa in the gardens at New Beginnings with wonderful effects.

Composting

In forests, meadows and other natural environments, organic debris, such as leaves and other plant bits, breaks down on the soil surface and the nutrients are gradually made available to the plants that are growing there. You can emulate that process in your own backyard with a compost pile. Compost is a great additive for your garden, and good composting methods will help reduce pest and disease problems.

Compost can be made in a pile, in a wooden box or in a purchased compost bin. Two methods can be used; neither is complicated, but one requires more effort.

If you use kitchen scraps, consider introducing red worms to the mix. You can have usable worm castings in as little as six weeks. The process is simple. Get a plastic container and ensure it has drainage holes. Place a light layer of shredded newspaper (avoid glossy newsprint) into the container and add all kitchen scraps, minus any meat products. You can buy red worms at any bait shop and let them eat your garbage.

Gardeners' best friends

Plastic composters

Wooden compost bins

Materials for compost

A compost pile or bin is a controlled environment where organic matter can be broken down before being introduced to your garden.

The 'active' or hot composting method requires you to turn the pile every week or so during the growing season. Frequent turning creates compost faster, but because the compost generates a lot of heat, some beneficial microorganisms that help fight diseases are killed. If you prefer the active approach to composting, several good books give step-by-step details of the process.

For most gardeners, the easier method, 'passive' or cold composting, is the more practical approach. Making a passive compost pile involves simply dumping most yard waste into a pile. This organic stuff may include weeds pulled from the garden, pruned materials cut into small pieces and leftover grass clippings and fall leaves. Grass clippings should be left on the lawn for the most part, but you can collect them every couple of weeks to add to the pile. Similarly, some fallen leaves should be chopped up with a mulching mower and left on the lawn; some can be collected and used directly as mulch under shrubs and on flowerbeds; and the remainder can be composted. Many gardeners collect leaves from neighbors, store them in plastic bags and add them to their compost pile over the following year.

Fruit and vegetable scraps may be added to the pile as well, but they attract small animals, which can be a nuisance. Do not put weed seeds or diseased or pest-ridden plants into your compost pile, or you risk spreading problems throughout your entire garden.

After a season or two, the passive pile will have at the bottom a layer of pure black gold, looking much like the leaf mold found in the woods. That is your finished compost. You get to it by moving the top of the pile aside. Spreading the finished compost on the surface of the garden bed will do good things for the soil. Because compost is usually in short supply, many gardeners just use it as an amendment when planting seedlings, perennials and small shrubs.

Many municipalities now recycle yard wastes into compost that is made available to residents. Contact your city hall to see if this valuable resource is available to you.

Whether you use your own or store-bought compost, add a trowelful of compost to the planting hole and mix it into the garden soil before planting your perennial.

Selecting Perennials

PERENNIALS CAN BE PURCHASED AS PLANTS OR SEEDS. PURCHASED plants may begin flowering the same year they are planted, while plants started from seed may take two to three years to mature. Starting plants from seed is more economical if you want large numbers of plants. (Read about starting perennials from seed in the Propagating Perennials section, p. 47.)

Plants and seeds are available from many sources. Garden centers, mail-order catalogs and even friends and neighbors are excellent sources of perennials.

A number of garden societies promote the exchange of seeds, and many public gardens sell seeds of rare plants. Gardening clubs are also a great source of rare and unusual plants.

Purchased plants come in two main forms. They are sold in pots or they are sold bare-root, usually packed in moist peat moss or sawdust. Potted perennials are growing and have probably been raised in the pot. Bare-root perennials are typically dormant, although some of the previous year's growth may be evident or there may be new growth starting. Sometimes the piece of root appears to have no evident growth, past or present. Both potted and bare-root perennials are good purchases, and in each case there are things to look for to make sure that you are getting a plant of the best quality.

Potted plants come in many sizes. Though a larger plant may appear more mature, it may be better to choose a smaller one that will suffer less from the shock of being transplanted. Since most perennials grow quickly once they are planted in the garden, the better buy may well be the smaller plant. Select plants that seem to be a good size for the pot they are in. When tapped lightly out of the pot, the roots should be visible but not winding and twisting around the inside of the pot. The leaves should be a healthy color.

If the leaves appear to be chewed or damaged, check carefully for insects or diseases. Do not purchase diseased plants. If you find insects on the plant, you may not want to purchase it unless you are willing to cope with the hitchhikers you are taking home. To avoid spreading the pest, deal with any pest problems before you move the plants into the garden. If you do see a diseased or infested plant in a nursery, tell the nursery workers, who will appreciate the information.

Once you get your plants home, water them if they are dry and keep them in a lightly shaded location until you plant them. Remove any damaged growth and discard it. Plant your new perennials into the garden as soon as possible.

Bare-root plants are most commonly sold through mail order, but some are available in garden centers, usually in the spring. Choose roots that are dormant (without top growth). If a bare-root plant has been trying to grow in the stressful conditions of a plastic bag, it may have too little energy to recover and may take longer to establish itself once planted in the garden.

Cut off any damaged parts of the roots with a very sharp knife. Bare-root perennials will dehydrate quickly out of soil, so they need to be planted more quickly than potted plants. Soak the roots in lukewarm water and plant them either directly in the garden or into pots with good quality potting soil until they can be moved to the garden.

Once you have planned your garden, prepared the soil and got the perennials ready, it is time to plant.

Overgrown, unhealthy plant on left, healthy selection on right

Planting Perennials

IF YOUR PERENNIALS HAVE identification tags, be sure to poke them into the soil next to the newly planted perennials. Next spring, when your perennial bed is nothing but a few stubs of green, the tags will help you with identification and remind you that there is indeed a plant in that bare patch of soil. Most of these tags include information on what care the plant needs. I often staple the tag on a small wooden bamboo stake and place it near the plant.

Potted Perennials

Perennials in pots are convenient because you can space them out across the bed or rearrange them before you start to dig. To prevent the roots from drying out, do not unpot the plant until immediately before you transplant.

To plant potted perennials, start by digging a hole about the width and depth of the pot. Remove the perennial from the pot. If the pot is small enough, you can hold your hand across the top of the pot, letting your fingers straddle the stem of the plant, and then turn it upside down. Never pull on the stem or leaves to get a plant out of a pot. It is better to cut a difficult pot off rather than risk damaging the plant. Tease a few roots out of the soil ball to get the plant growing in the right direction. If the roots have become densely wound around the inside of the pot, you should cut into or score

I once asked an internationally known Japanese landscaper what he did to arrange his plants. 'I do three rock,' he told me. 'Three rock?' I asked. 'I'll show you.' He turned his back on the landscape and tossed three shiny rocks behind him. He then instructed the laborers to put the plants where the rocks landed. Maybe this wasn't too scientific, but he was getting paid very well for it. I've been a three and five rock person ever since.

the root mass with a sharp knife to encourage new growth into the surrounding soil. The process of cutting into the bottom half of the root ball and spreading the two halves of the mass outward like butterfly wings is called 'butterflying the roots' and is a very effective way to promote fast growth of pot-bound perennials that are being transplanted. Place the plant into the prepared hole. It should be buried to the same level that it was at in the pot, or a little higher, to allow for the soil to settle. If the plant is too low in the ground, it may rot when rain collects around

the crown. Fill the soil in around the roots and firm it down. Water the plant well as soon as you have planted it and regularly until it has established itself.

Bare-root Perennials

Bare-root perennials should not be spaced out across the bed unless they are already in pots. Roots dry out very quickly if you leave them lying about waiting to be planted. If you want to visualize your spacing, you can poke sticks into the ground or put rocks down to represent the locations of your perennials.

Support the plant as you remove it from the pot.

Gently loosen the rootball before firming it into the soil.

If you have been keeping your bare-root perennials in potting soil, you may find that the roots have not grown enough to knit the soil together and that all the soil falls away from the root when you remove it from the pot. Don't be concerned. Simply follow the regular root-planting instructions. If the soil does hold together, plant the root the way you would a potted perennial.

The type of hole you need to dig will depend on the type of roots the bare-root perennial has. Plants with **fibrous roots** will need a mound of soil in the center of the planting hole over which the roots can be spread out evenly. The hole should be dug as deep as the longest roots. Mound the soil into the center of the hole up to ground level. Spread the roots out around the mound and cover them with loosened soil. If you are adding just one or two plants and do not want to prepare an entire bed, dig a hole twice as wide and deep as the root ball and amend the soil with composted manure mixed with peat

moss or planting mix. Add a slow-release organic fertilizer to the backfill of soil that you spread around the plant. Fresh chicken or barnyard manure can also be used to improve small areas, but it should not be placed in the planting hole. Place only a small amount on top of the soil where it can leach into the soil. This way you will not expose the roots of the plant to fertilizer burn.

Plants with a **taproot** need to be planted in a hole that is narrow and about as deep as the root is long. Use a trowel to open up a suitable hole, tuck the root into it and fill it in again with the soil around it. If you can't tell which end is up, plant the root on its side.

Some plants have what appear to be taproots, but the plant seems to be growing off the side of the root rather than upwards from one end. These are called **rhizomes**. Rhizomes are actually modified underground stems. Irises grow from rhizomes. Rhizomes should be planted horizontally in a shallow hole and covered with soil.

In most cases, you should try to get the crown of the plant at or just above soil level and loosen the surrounding soil in the planting hole. Keep the roots thoroughly watered until the plants are well established.

Whether the plants are potted or bare-root, it is good to leave them alone and let them recover from the stress of planting. In the first month, you will need only to water the plant regularly, weed around it and watch for pests. A mulch spread on the bed around your plants will keep in moisture and control weeds.

Always water in new plantings.

If you have prepared your beds properly, you probably won't have to fertilize in the first year. If you do want to fertilize, wait until your new plants have started healthy new growth, and apply only a weak fertilizer to avoid damaging the new root growth.

Planters

Perennials can also be grown in planters for portable displays that can be moved about the garden. Planters can also be used on patios or decks, in gardens with very poor soil or in yards where kids and dogs might destroy a traditional perennial bed. Many perennials such as plantain lilies and daylilies can grow in the same container without any fresh potting soil for five or six years. Be sure to fertilize and water perennials in planters more often than those growing in the ground. Dig your finger deep into the soil around the perennial to see if it needs water. Too much water in the planter causes root rot.

Always use a good quality potting mix or a soil mix intended for containers in your planters. Garden soil quickly loses its structure when used in a container and becomes a solid lump, preventing air, water and roots from penetrating into the soil. Plants will never thrive in a container if planted in soil from the garden. At the very least mix half garden soil with half peat moss and mix the two together well. However, trying to extend your potting soil with garden soil can often lead to disappointment.

When designing a planter garden, you can either keep one type of perennial in each planter and display

Mixed annuals and perennials

many planters together or mix different perennials in large planters along with annuals and bulbs. The latter choice results in a dynamic bouquet of flowers and foliage. Keep the tall upright perennials such as yarrow in the center of the planter, the rounded or bushy types such as coreopsis around the sides and low-growing or draping perennials such as candytuft along the edge of the planter. Perennials that have long bloom times or attractive foliage are good for planters.

Choose hardy perennials that can tolerate difficult conditions. Planters can be exposed to extremes of our variable weather. Perennials in planters dry out quickly in hot weather and become waterlogged after a couple of rainy days. Not all perennials are tough enough to survive in these extreme conditions. Some of the more invasive perennials are a good choice for planters because their spread is controlled but at the same time they are very tough to kill.

Because the exposed sides of a container provide little insulation for roots and containers allow for greater fluctuations in temperature, perennials in planters are more susceptible to damage from temperature extremes. The container itself may even crack if exposed to freezing temperatures. If you see a real cold snap coming on, the simplest thing you can do is move the planter to a sheltered spot. Many perennials do require some cold in the winter in order to flower the next year, so find a spot that is still cold but provides some shelter. Most container gardens take the winter quite well, except that if the containers sit in trays, the excessive water can rot the roots.

Before you plant your perennials, the pots can be insulated to protect the plants from excessive summer heat. Layer styrofoam insulation or 'packing peanuts' at the bottom of the pot and around the inside of the planter before you add your soil and plants. Make sure excess water can still drain freely from the container. Commercial planter-insulating materials are available at garden centers. This insulation will also protect the roots. Another method of protecting plants in containers from excessive heat is to water them more.

Perennials for Planters

Anemone (tuberous)
Beard Tongue
Blue Eyes
Candytuft
Catmint
Daylily
Dianthus
Geranium
Lady's Mantle
Peruvian Lily
Pincushion Flower
Plantain Lily
Stonecrop
Wallflower
Yarrow

Caring for Perennials

MANY PERENNIALS REQUIRE little care, but all will benefit from a few maintenance basics. Weeding, watering and grooming are just a few of the chores that, when done on a regular basis, keep major work to a minimum.

Weeding

Controlling weeds is one of the most important things you have to do in your garden. Weeds compete with your perennials for light, nutrients and space. Weeds can also harbor pests and diseases. Try to prevent weeds from germinating. If they do germinate, pull them out while they are still small and before they have a chance to flower, set seed and start a whole new generation of problems.

Weeds can be pulled out by hand or with a hoe. Quickly scuffing across the soil surface with the hoe will pull out small weeds and sever larger ones from their roots. A layer of mulch is an excellent way to suppress weeds.

Mulching

Mulches are an important gardening tool. They prevent weed seeds from germinating by blocking out the light. If small weeds do pop up in a mulched bed, they are very easy to pull. Soil temperatures remain more consistent and more moisture is retained under a layer of mulch. Mulch also prevents soil erosion

Weeds and tools

Mulched garden

during heavy rain or strong winds. Organic mulches can consist of compost, bark chips, shredded leaves or grass clippings. Organic mulches are desirable because they improve the soil and add nutrients as they break down. Shredded newspaper also makes a wonderful mulch. Shredded cedar bark or redwood bark has an added bonus of a naturally occuring fungicide that can help prevent root rot.

In spring, spread about 2–4" of mulch over your perennial beds around your plants. Keep the area immediately around the crown or stem of your plants clear. Mulch that is too close to your plants can trap moisture and prevent good air circulation, encouraging disease. If the layer of mulch disappears into the soil over summer, replenish it.

If you have tender perennials, mulching over winter is necessary. A 2–3" layer of shredded cedar bark or other organic material should be sufficient for protection. In late winter or early spring, once the weather starts to warm up, pull the mulch

layer off the plants and see if they have started growing. If they have, you can pull the mulch back, but keep it nearby in case you need to put it back on to protect the tender new growth from a late frost. Once your plants are well on their way and you are no longer worried about frost, you can remove the protective mulch completely. Compost the old mulch and apply a new spring and summer mulch.

Watering

Watering is another basic of perennial care. Many perennials need little supplemental watering if they have been planted in their preferred conditions and are given a moisture-retaining mulch. The rule of watering is to water thoroughly and infrequently. Plants given a light sprinkle of water every day will develop roots that stay close to the soil surface, making the plants vulnerable to heat and dry spells. Watering deeply (at least 4") into the soil once a week will allow plants to develop a deeper root system. In a dry spell or heat snap, they will be adapted to seeking out the water trapped deeper in the ground.

It is best to do the majority of your watering in the morning. This allows any moisture on the plant to dry during the day, lessening the chances of fungal diseases developing on the plant.

To avoid overwatering, check the amount of moisture in the rootzone before applying any water. You can feel the surface or poke your finger into the top 1–2" of soil. You can also try rolling a bit of the soil from around the plant into a ball. If the soil forms a ball, it is moist and needs no extra water.

To save time, money and water you may wish to install an irrigation system. Irrigation systems apply the water exactly where it is needed, near the roots, and reduce the amount of water lost to evaporation. They can be very complex or very simple depending on your needs. A simple irrigation system would involve laying soaker hoses around your garden beds under the mulch. Consult your local garden centers or landscape professionals for more information.

Perennials in containers or planters will probably need to be watered more frequently than plants growing in the ground. The smaller the container, the more often the plants will need watering. Containers may need to be watered twice daily during hot, sunny weather. If the soil in your container dries out, you will have to water several times to make sure water is absorbed throughout the planting medium.

Dig into the soil, and if it is dry at all, water more. There is a product on the market in Northern California called Water-in™, which can help water penetrate into dry soils. This is usually added to peat moss and soil mixes to help them to keep their water-holding abilities.

Fertilizing

If you prepare your beds well and add new compost to them each spring, you should not need to add extra fertilizer. If you have a limited amount of compost, you can mix a slow-release fertilizer into the soil around your perennials in the spring. Some plants; e.g., candle larkspurs, are heavy feeders that need additional supplements throughout the growing season.

There are many organic and chemical fertilizers available at garden centers. Be sure to use the recommended quantity because too much fertilizer will do more harm than good. Roots can be burned by fertilizer that is applied in high concentrations. Problems are more likely to be caused by chemical fertilizers because they are more concentrated than organic fertilizers.

Compost Tea
Mix 1 to 2 pounds of compost in 5 gallons of water. Let sit for 4–7 days. For use, dilute the mix until it resembles weak tea. Apply as a foliar spray or use during normal watering.

Aster (above), Purple Coneflower (center)

Sedum 'Autumn Joy' (below)

Grooming

Many perennials benefit from grooming. Resilient plants, plentiful blooming and compact growth are the signs of a well-groomed garden. Pinching, thinning, disbudding, staking and deadheading plants will enhance the beauty of a perennial garden. The methods are simple, but you will have to experiment in order to get the right effect in your own garden.

Thinning is done to clump-forming perennials such as black-eyed Susan, purple coneflower or bee balm early in the year when shoots have just emerged. These plants develop a dense clump of stems that allows very little air or light into the center of the plant. Remove half the shoots when they first emerge to increase air circulation and prevent diseases such as powdery mildew. The increased light encourages more compact growth and more flowers. Growth that is affecting plant shape or is weak or diseased may need to be thinned throughout the growing season.

Trimming or **pinching** perennials is a simple procedure, but timing it correctly and achieving just the right look can be tricky. Early in the year, before the flower buds have appeared, trim the plant to encourage new side shoots. Remove the tip and some stems of the plant just above a leaf or pair of leaves. This can be done stem by stem, but if you have a lot of plants you can trim off the tops with your hedge shears to one-third of the height you expect the plants to reach. The growth that begins to emerge can be pinched again. Beautiful layered effects can be achieved by staggering the trimming times by a week or two.

Perennials to Trim Early in the Season

Aster
Bee Balm
Black-eyed Susan
Catmint
Hibiscus
Lavender Cotton
Mallow
Purple Coneflower
Sedum 'Autumn Joy'

Give plants enough time to set buds and flower. Continual pinching will encourage very dense growth but also delay flowering. Most spring-flowering plants cannot be pinched back or they will not flower. Early summer or mid-summer bloomers should be pinched only once, as early in the season as possible. Late summer and fall bloomers can be pinched several times but should be left alone past June. Don't pinch the plant if flower buds have formed—it may not have enough energy or time left in the year to develop a new set of buds. Experimenting and keeping detailed notes will improve your pinching skills.

Disbudding is another grooming stage. This is the removal of some flower buds to encourage the remaining ones to produce larger flowers. This technique is popular with peony growers and growers who enter plants in fairs or similar flower competitions.

Staking, the use of poles or wires to hold plants erect, can often be avoided by astute thinning and pinching, but there are always a few plants that will need support to look their best in your garden. There are three basic types of stakes used for the different growth habits that need support. Plants that develop tall spikes such as hollyhocks, candle larkspurs and sometimes foxgloves require each spike to be staked individually. A strong narrow pole such as a bamboo stick can be pushed into the ground early in the year and the spike tied to the stake as it grows. Ensure the plant is securely tied with plant-friendly ties such as soft, stretchable material or strips of thin plastic, such as plastic grocery bags or plastic wrap. A forked branch can also be used to support single-stem plants.

Ripe seed clusters atop Meadowsweet

branches inserted into the ground around the young plants; the plants then grow up into the twigs.

Some people consider stakes to be unsightly no matter how hidden they seem to be. There are a few things you can do to reduce the need for staking. First, grow the plant in the right conditions. Don't assume a plant will do better in a richer soil than is recommended. Very rich soil causes many plants to produce weak, leggy growth that is prone to falling over. Also, a plant that likes full sun will be stretched out and leggy if grown in the shade. Second, use other plants for support. Mix plants that have a stable structure with plants that need support. A plant may still fall over slightly, but only as far as its neighbor will allow. Finally, look for compact varieties that don't require staking.

Deadheading, the removal of flowers once they are finished blooming, serves several purposes. It keeps plants looking tidy, prevents the plant from spreading seeds (and therefore seedlings) throughout the garden, often prolongs blooming and helps prevent pest and disease problems.

Deadheading is not necessary for every plant. Seedheads of some plants are left in place to provide interest in the garden over winter. Other plants, such as hollyhock, are short-lived, and leaving some of the seedheads in place encourages future generations to replace the old plants. In some cases the self-sown seedlings do not possess the attractive features of the parent plant. Deadheading may be required in these cases.

Many plants, such as peonies, get a bit top heavy as they grow and tend to flop over once they reach a certain height. A wire hoop, sometimes called a peony ring, is the most unobtrusive way to hold up such a plant. When the plant is young, the legs of the peony ring are pushed into the ground around it, and as the plant grows, it is supported by the wire ring. At the same time, the bushy growth hides the ring. Wire tomato cages can also be used to support peonies.

Other plants, such as coreopsis, form a floppy tangle of stems. These plants can be supported with twiggy

Perennials with Interesting Seedheads
Astilbe
Bear's Breeches
Bee Balm
Euphorbia
Globe Thistle
Meadowsweet
Oriental Poppy
Purple Coneflower
Sea Holly
Sea Pink
Sedum 'Autumn Joy'

Perennials that Self-seed
Balloon Flower
Bleeding Heart (variable seedlings)
Cardinal Flower
Columbine
Dianthus
Evening Primrose
Foxglove
Hollyhock (variable seedlings)
Lady's Mantle
Lupine
Mallow
Sandwort
Violet

Foxglove (above), Mallow (below)

Flowers can be deadheaded by hand or snipped off with hand pruners. Bushy plants that have many tiny flowers, particularly ones that have a short bloom period, can be more aggressively pruned back with garden shears once they have completed their bloom cycle. For some plants—such as Creeping Phlox—shearing will promote new growth and possibly encourage blooms later in the season.

Basket-of-gold with tulips

Perennials to Shear Back after Blooming
Basket-of-gold
Bellflower
Bidens
Blue Star Flower
Candytuft
Creeping Phlox
False Rockcress
Geranium
Golden Marguerite
Lithodora
Sweet Woodruff
Thyme
Yarrow

Here are some of my favorite fertilizers. VF 11™ is a liquid that can be added to every watering. It can also be sprayed on the foliage on a weekly basis. Don't worry that the fertilizer concentration is so light. I have found that less is better. Formulas that contain large amounts of chemicals are a waste because the plant can't use them right away. Chicken manure is better than other animal fertilizers for working into the soil. Alfalfa pellets contain triacontanol, which is a very powerful plant growth hormone. It stimulates the roots of plants so that they actually use the fertilizer you give them. Bone meal is touted as a wonderful fertilizer for bulbs. Unfortunately it attracts animals to the planted location and can cause major destruction. Fish emulsion is great to use as a liquid. I apply it at one-third the recommended rate. This way you can use it more often without the danger of burning the plant.

Propagating Perennials

PROPAGATING YOUR OWN PERENNIALS IS AN INTERESTING AND challenging aspect of gardening that can save you money but also requires time and space. Seeds, cuttings and divisions are the three methods of increasing your perennial population. There are benefits and problems associated with each method.

Seeds

Starting perennials from seed is a great way to propagate a large number of plants at a relatively low cost. Seeds can be purchased or collected from your own or a friend's perennial garden. There are some limitations to propagating from seed. Some cultivars and varieties don't pass on their desirable traits to their offspring. Other perennials have seeds that take a very long time to germinate, if they germinate at all, and may take an even longer time to grow to flowering size. However, many perennials grow easily from seed and flower within a year or two of being transplanted

into the garden. There are challenges and limitations to starting perennials from seed, but the work will be worth it when you see the plants you raised from tiny seedlings finally begin to flower.

Specific propagation information is given for each plant, but there are a few basic rules for starting all seeds. Some seeds can be started directly in the garden, but it is easier to control temperature and moisture levels and to provide a sterile environment if you start the seeds indoors. Seeds can be started in pots or, if you need a lot of plants, flats. Use a sterile soil mix intended for starting seeds. The soil will generally need to be kept moist but not soggy. Most seeds germinate in moderately warm temperatures of about 57–70° F.

There are many seed-starting supplies available at garden centers. Some supplies are useful but many are not necessary. Seed-tray dividers are useful. These dividers, often called plug trays, are made of plastic and prevent the roots from tangling with the roots of the other plants and from being disturbed when seedlings are transplanted. Heating coils or pads can be useful. Placed under the pots or flats, they keep the soil at a constant temperature.

All seedlings are susceptible to a problem called 'damping off,' which is caused by soil-borne fungi. An afflicted seedling looks as though someone has pinched the stem at soil level, causing the plant to topple over. The pinched area blackens and the seedling dies. Sterile soil mix, good air circulation and evenly moist soil will help prevent this problem. Spreading a 1/4" layer of peat moss over the seed bed can also reduce the possibility of damping off.

Fill your pot or seed tray with the soil mix and firm it down slightly—not too firmly or the soil will not drain. Wet the soil before planting your seeds. Seeds may wash into clumps if the soil is watered after the seeds are planted. Large seeds can be placed individually and spaced out

Prepared seed tray

Misting seeded tray

Seeding tiny seeds

Seeded pot covered with plastic

in pots or trays. If you have divided inserts for your trays, you can plant one or two seeds per section. Small seeds may have to be sprinkled in a bit more randomly. Fold a sheet of paper in half and place the small seeds in the crease. Gently tap the underside of the fold to roll the seeds off the paper in a controlled manner. Some seeds are so tiny that they look like dust. These seeds can be mixed with a small quantity of very fine sand and spread on the soil surface. These tiny seeds may not need to be covered with any more soil. The medium-sized seeds can be lightly covered and the larger seeds can be pressed into the soil and then lightly covered. Do not cover seeds that need to be exposed to light in order to germinate. Water the seeds using a very fine spray if the soil starts to dry out. A hand-held spray bottle will moisten the soil without disturbing the seeds.

The amount and timing of watering is critical to successful growing from seed. Most germinated seed and young seedlings will perish if the soil is allowed to dry out. Strive to maintain a consistently moist soil, which may mean watering lightly 2–3 times a day. As the seedlings get bigger you can cut back on the number of times you have to water but you will have to water a little heavier each time. A rule of thumb is when the seedlings have their first true leaves, you can cut back to watering once a day.

Plant only one type of seed in each pot or flat. Each species has a different rate of germination, and the germinated seedlings will

Candle Larkspur and Peruvian Lily in mixed bed (above)

Lupine (center), Oriental Poppy (below)

Himalayan Poppy (above), Phlox (below)

require different conditions than the seeds that have yet to germinate. To keep the environment moist, you can place pots inside clear plastic bags. Change the bag or turn it inside out once the condensation starts to build up and drip. Plastic bags can be held up with stakes or wires poked in around the edges of the pot. Many seed trays come with clear plastic covers which can be placed over the flats to keep the moisture in. Plastic can be removed once the seeds have germinated.

Seeds generally do not require a lot of light in order to germinate, so pots or trays can be kept in a warm, out of the way place. Once the seeds have germinated, they can be placed in a bright location but out of direct sun. Plants should be transplanted to individual pots once they have three or four true leaves. True leaves are the ones that look like the mature leaves. (The first one or two leaves are actually part of the seed.) Plants in plug trays can be left until neighboring leaves start to touch each other. At this point the plants will be competing for light and should be transplanted to individual pots.

Young seedlings do not need to be fertilized. Fertilizer will cause seedlings to produce soft, spindly growth that is susceptible to attack by insects and diseases. The seed itself provides all the nutrition the seedling will need. A fertilizer diluted to one-quarter strength can be used once seedlings have four or five true leaves. Organic fertilizers are safer to use because they do not burn and need to be used less often.

Perennials to Start from Seed

California Poppy
Candle Larkspur
Coreopsis
Dianthus
Foxglove
Himalayan Poppy
Lady's Mantle
Lupine
Mallow
Oriental Poppy
Peruvian Lily
Phlox
Pincushion Flower
Rock Cress

California Poppy (above), Coreopsis (below)

Seeds have protective devices that prevent them from germinating when conditions are not favorable or from all germinating at once. In the wild, staggered germination periods improve the chances of survival. Many seeds will easily grow as soon as they are planted, but others need to have their defenses lowered before they will germinate. Some seeds also produce poisonous chemicals in the seed coats to deter insects.

Seeds can be tricked into thinking the conditions are right for sprouting. Some thick-coated seeds can be soaked for a day or two in a glass of water to promote germination. This mimics the end of the dry season and the beginning of the rainy season, which is when the plant would germinate in its natural environment. The water softens the seed coat and in some cases washes away the chemicals that have been preventing germination.

Other thick-coated seeds need to have their seed coats scratched to allow moisture to penetrate the seed coat and prompt germination. In nature, birds scratch the seeds with gravel in their craws and acid in their stomachs. Nick the seeds with a knife or file, or gently rub them between two sheets of sand paper. Leave the seeds in a dry place for a day or so after scratching them before planting to give the seeds a chance to get ready for germination before they are exposed to water. Lupines and anemones have seeds that need their thick coats scratched.

Plants from northern climates often have seeds that wait until spring before they germinate. These seeds must be exposed to a period of cold, which mimics winter, before they will germinate. One method of cold treatment is to plant the seeds in a pot or tray and place them in the refrigerator for up to two months. Check the container regularly and don't allow these to dry out. This method is fairly simple but not very practical if your refrigerator is crowded. Yarrow and bergenia have seeds that respond to cold treatment.

A less space-consuming method is to mix the seeds with some moistened sand, peat or sphagnum moss. Place the mix in a sealable sandwich bag and pop it in the refrigerator for up to two months, again being sure the sand or moss doesn't dry out. The seeds can then be planted into a pot or tray. Spread the seeds and the

Trim cutting

Dip cut end into rooting hormone

Firm cutting into rooting media

Rooted cuttings

moist sand or moss onto the prepared surface and press it all down
gently.

A cold frame is a wonderful tool
for the gardener. It can be used to
protect tender plants over winter, to
start vegetable seeds early in spring,
to harden plants off before moving
them to the garden, to protect fall-
germinating seedlings and young
cuttings or divisions and to start
seeds that need a cold treatment.
This mini-greenhouse structure is
built so that ground level on the
inside of the cold frame is lower
than on the outside. The angled,
hinged lid is fitted with glass. The
soil around the outside of the cold
frame insulates the plants inside.
The lid lets light in and collects
some heat during the day and prevents rain from damaging tender
plants. If the interior gets too hot,
the lid can be raised for ventilation.

Preparing seeds for cold treatment (above)

Cuttings

Cuttings are an excellent way to
propagate varieties and cultivars
that you really like but that don't
come true from seed or don't produce seed at all. Each cutting will
grow into a reproduction (clone) of
the parent plant. Cuttings are taken
from the stems of some perennials
and the roots of others.

Stem cuttings are generally taken
in spring and early summer. During
this time plants go through a flush
of fresh, new growth, either before
or after flowering. Generally, stem
cuttings are more successful and
quicker to grow if you include the
tip of the stem in the cutting. Avoid
taking cuttings from plants that are

Scratching seed coat (center), cold frame (below)

Bellflower (above), Lithodora (center)

Yarrow (below)

in flower. Plants that are in flower, or are about to flower, are busy trying to reproduce; plants that are busy growing, by contrast, are already full of the right hormones to promote quick root growth. If you do take cuttings from plants that are flowering, be sure to remove the flowers and the buds to divert the plant's energy back into growing.

Large numbers of cuttings don't often result in as many plants. Also, cuttings need to be kept in a warm humid place, which makes them prone to fungal diseases. Providing proper sanitation and encouraging quick rooting will increase the survival rate of your cuttings. Dusting with soil sulfur will reduce the incidence of fungal disease.

Perennials to Propagate from Stem Cuttings
Aster
Basket-of-gold
Beard Tongue
Bellflower
Bleeding Heart
Candytuft
Dianthus
Dusty Miller
Euphorbia
False Rockcress
Lithodora
Salvia
Sedum 'Autumn Joy'
Thyme
Violet
Wallflower
Yarrow

There is disagreement over what size cuttings should be. Some gardeners claim that smaller cuttings are more likely to root and will root more quickly. Other gardeners claim that larger cuttings develop more roots and become established more quickly once planted in the garden. You may wish to try different sizes to see what works best for you. Generally, a small cutting is 1–2" long and a large cutting is 4–6" long.

Another way to determine the size of cuttings is to count the leaf nodes on the cutting. You will want at least three or four nodes on a cutting. The node is where the leaf joins the stem and where the new roots and leaves will grow from. The base of the cutting will be just below a node. Strip the leaves gently from the first and second nodes and plant the cutting so the first and second nodes are beneath the soil surface. The new stems and leaves will grow from the nodes above the soil. The leaves can be left in place on the cutting above ground. If there is a lot of space between nodes, your cutting will be longer than the guidelines mentioned above. Some plants have almost no space at all between nodes. Cut these plants to the recommended length and gently remove the leaves from the lower half of the cutting. Plants with several nodes close together often root quickly and abundantly.

Always use a sharp, sterile knife to make the cuttings. Cuts should be made straight across the stem. Once you have stripped the leaves, you can dip the end of the cutting into

False Rockcress (above), Dianthus (below)

Beard Tongue (above), Salvia (center)

Candytuft edging a mixed border (below)

a rooting-hormone powder intended for softwood cuttings. Sprinkle the powder onto a piece of paper and dip the cuttings into it. Discard any extra powder left on the paper to prevent the spread of disease. Tap or blow the extra powder off the cutting. Cuttings caked with rooting hormone are more likely to rot rather than root and they do not root any faster than those that are lightly dusted. Your cuttings are now prepared for planting.

Although the above method is preferred, many gardeners have had success keeping their cuttings in water. Using dark containers instead of clear containers produces the best results.

The sooner you plant your cuttings the better. The less water the cuttings lose, the less likely they are to wilt and the more quickly they will root. Cuttings can be planted in a similar manner to seeds. Use sterile soil mix, intended for seeds or cuttings, or use sterilized sand, perlite, vermiculite or a combination of the three. Firm the soil down and moisten it before you start planting. Poke a hole in the surface of the soil with a pencil or similar object, tuck the cutting in and gently firm the soil around it. Make sure the lowest leaves do not touch the soil and that the cuttings are spaced far enough apart that adjoining leaves do not touch each other.

Use pots or trays that can be covered with plastic to keep in the humidity. If you use a plastic bag, push stakes or wires into the soil around the edge of the pot so that the plastic will be held off the leaves.

The rigid plastic lids that are available for trays may not be high enough to fit over the cuttings in which case you will have to use stakes and a plastic bag to cover the tray.

Keep the cuttings in a warm place, about 65–70° F, in bright indirect light. A couple of holes poked in the bag will create some ventilation. Turn the bag inside out when condensation becomes heavy. Keep the soil moist. A hand-held mister will gently moisten the soil without disturbing the cuttings.

Most cuttings will require from one to four weeks to root. After two weeks, give the cutting a gentle tug. You will feel resistance if roots have formed. If the cutting feels as though it can pull out of the soil, then gently push it back down and leave it a while longer. New growth is also a good sign that your cutting has rooted. Some gardeners simply leave the cuttings alone until they can see roots through the holes in the bottoms of the pots. Uncover the cuttings once they have developed roots.

Apply a foliar feed when the cuttings are showing new leaf growth. Plants quickly absorb nutrients through the leaves; by using a foliar fertilizer, you can avoid stressing the newly formed roots. Your local garden center should have foliar fertilizers and information about applying them. You can use your hand-held mister to apply foliar fertilizers.

Once your cuttings are rooted and have established themselves, they can be potted individually. If you

Bee Balm (above),
Stonecrop with Hens and Chicks (below)

Ivy-leaved Geranium (above), Daylily (center)

Lupine (below)

rooted several cuttings in one pot or tray, you may find that the roots have tangled together. If gentle pulling doesn't separate them, take the entire clump that is tangled together and try rinsing some of the soil away. This should free the roots enough for you to separate the plants.

Pot the young plants in a sterile potting soil. They can be moved into a sheltered area of the garden or a cold frame and grown in pots until they are large enough to plant in the garden. The plants may need some protection over the first winter in the coldest areas of the state. Keep them in the cold frame if they are still in pots. Give them an extra layer of mulch if they have been transplanted into the garden.

Basal cuttings involve removing the new growth from the main clump and rooting it in the same manner as stem cuttings. Many plants send up new shoots or plantlets around their bases. Often, the plantlets will already have a few roots growing. The young plants develop quickly and may even grow to flowering size the first summer. You may have to cut back some of the top growth of the shoot because the tiny developing roots won't be able to support a lot of top growth. Treat these cuttings in the same way you would a stem cutting. Use a sterile knife to cut out the shoot. Sterile soil mix and humid conditions are preferred. Pot plants individually or place them in soft soil in the garden until new growth appears and roots have developed.

Perennials to Start from Basal Cuttings

Bee Balm
Bellflower
Candle Larkspur
Catmint
Daylily
Euphorbia
Gaura
Geranium
Gunnera
Hens and Chicks
Lupine
Mallow
Phlox
Pincushion Flower
Stonecrop

Root cuttings can also be taken from some plants. Dandelions are often inadvertently propagated this way: even the smallest piece of root left in the ground can sprout a new plant, foiling every attempt to eradicate them from lawns and flower beds. But there are perennials that have this ability as well. The main difference between starting root cuttings and stem cuttings is that the root cuttings must be kept fairly dry because they can rot very easily.

Cuttings can be taken from the fleshy roots of certain perennials that do not propagate well from stem cuttings. These cuttings should be taken in early or mid-spring when the ground is just starting to warm up and the roots are just about to break dormancy. At this time, the roots of the perennials are full of nutrients that the plants stored the previous summer and fall, and hormones are initiating growth. You may have to wet the soil around

Gunnera (above), Catmint (below)

Black-Eyed Susan (above), Anenome (center)

Sea Pink (below)

the plant so that you can loosen it enough to get to the roots.

Keep the roots slightly moist, but not wet, while you are rooting them, and keep track of which end is up. Roots must be planted in a vertical, not horizontal, position in the soil, and roots need to be kept in the orientation they held while previously attached to the parent plant. There are different tricks people use to differentiate the top from the bottom of the roots. One method is to cut straight across the tops and diagonally across the bottoms.

You do not want very young or very old roots. Very young roots are usually white and quite soft; very old roots are tough and woody. The roots you should use will be tan in color and still fleshy. To prepare your root, cut out the section you will be using with a sterile knife. (Sterilize a knife by dipping it in denatured alcohol or a 10% bleach solution.) Cut the root into 1–2" long pieces. Remove any side roots before planting the sections in pots or planting trays. You can use the same type of soil mix as for seeds and stem cuttings. Poke the pieces vertically into the soil and leave a tiny bit of the end poking up out of the soil.

Keep the pots or trays in a warm place out of direct sunlight. Avoid overwatering them. They will send up new shoots once they have rooted and can be planted in the same manner as stem cuttings (see p. 53).

Perennials to Propagate from Root Cuttings

Anenome
Baby's Breath
Black-eyed Susan
Bleeding Heart
Columbine
Evening Primrose
Gunnera
Oriental Poppy
Phlox
Sea Holly

Rhizomes are the easiest root-type cuttings with which to propagate plants. Rhizomes are thick, fleshy root-like stems that grow horizontally just under the soil. Periodically, they send up new shoots from along the length of the rhizome. In this way the plant spreads. It is easy to take advantage of this feature. Take rhizome cuttings when the plant is growing vigorously, usually in the late spring or early summer.

Dig up a section of rhizome. If you look closely at it you will see that it appears to be growing in sections. The places where these sections join are called nodes. It is from these nodes that feeder roots (smaller stringy roots) extend down and new plants sprout up. You may even see that small plants are already sprouting. Cut the rhizome into pieces. Each piece should have at least one of these nodes in it.

Fill a pot or planting tray to about 1" from the top of the container with perlite, vermiculite or seeding soil. Moisten the soil and let the excess water drain away. Lay the rhizome pieces flat on top of the mix and almost cover them with more of the soil mix. Leaving a bit of the top exposed to the light will encourage the shoots to sprout. The soil does not have to be kept consistently wet; to avoid rot, let your rhizome dry out between waterings. Once your cuttings have established themselves, they can be potted individually and grown in the same manner as stem cuttings (see p. 53).

Stolons are similar to rhizomes except that they grow horizontally on the soil surface. They can be treated in the same way as rhizomes.

Perennials to Propagate from Rhizomes

Bellflower
Bergenia
Geranium
Iris

Divisions

Division is quite possibly the easiest way to propagate perennials. As most perennials grow, they form larger and larger clumps. Dividing this clump once it gets big will rejuvenate the plant, keep its size in check and provide you with more plants. If a plant you really want is expensive, consider buying only one because within a few years you may have more than you can handle.

How often a perennial needs dividing or can be divided will vary. Some perennials, such as astilbe, need dividing almost every year to keep them vigorous, while others, such as peonies, should never be divided, because they dislike having their roots disturbed. Each perennial entry in the book gives recommendations for division. In general, watch for several signs that a perennial should be divided:

- the center of the plant has died out
- the plant is no longer flowering as profusely as it did in previous years
- the plant is encroaching on the growing space of other plants sharing the bed.

It is relatively easy to divide perennials. Begin by digging up the entire clump and knocking any large clods of soil away from the root ball. The clump can then be split into several pieces. A small plant with fibrous roots can be torn into sections by hand. A large plant can be pried apart with a pair of garden forks inserted back to back into the clump. Plants with thicker tuberous or rhizomatous roots can be cut into sections with a sharp, sterile knife. In all cases, cut away any old sections that have died out and re-plant only the newer, more vigorous sections.

Once your original clump is divided into sections, re-plant one or two of them into the original location. Take this opportunity to work organic matter into the soil where the perennial was growing before re-planting it. The other sections can be moved to new spots in the garden or potted and given away to friends and neighbors. Get the sections back into the ground as quickly as possible to prevent the exposed roots from drying out. Plan where you are going to plant your divisions and have the spots prepared before you start digging up. Plant your perennial divisions in pots if you aren't sure where to put them all. Water new transplants thoroughly and keep them well watered until they have re-established themselves.

The larger the sections of the division, the more quickly the plant will re-establish itself and grow to blooming size again. For example, a perennial divided into four sections will bloom sooner than one divided into ten sections. Very small divisions may benefit from being planted in pots until they are bigger and better able to fend for themselves in the garden.

Newly planted divisions will need extra care and attention when they are first planted. They will need regular watering and, for the first few days, shade from direct sunlight. A light covering of burlap or damp newspaper should be sufficient to shelter them for this short period. Divisions that have been planted in pots should be moved to a shaded location.

There is some debate about the best time to divide perennials. Some gardeners prefer to divide perennials while they are dormant, whereas others feel perennials establish themselves more quickly if divided when they are growing vigorously. You may wish to experiment with dividing at different times of the year to see what works best for you. If you do divide perennials while they are growing, you will need to cut back one-third to one-half of the growth so as not to stress the roots while they are repairing the damage done to them.

Sometimes if the center of a perennial dies out, it can be rejuvenated without digging up the whole plant. Dig out the center of the plant, ensuring you remove all of the dead and weak growth. Replace the soil you removed with fresh planting mix. Sprinkle a small amount of alfalfa pellets on top of the fresh planting mix. The center of the plant should fill in quickly.

Some perennials do not like to be divided, do not need to be divided or perform best when they are undisturbed. Many of these can be reproduced by taking side shoots from the mother plant. These side shoots are easily rooted in planting mix. Often the side shoots may have already developed rudimentary roots.

Non-dividing Perennials
Baby's Breath
Balloon Flower
Butterfly Weed
Euphorbia
Lady's Mantle
Lupine
Oriental Poppy
Peony
Russian Sage

Butterfly Weed (above), Balloon Flower (center)

Lady's Mantle (below)

Problems & Pests

PERENNIAL GARDENS ARE BOTH AN ASSET AND A LIABILITY WHEN it comes to pests and diseases. Many insects and diseases attack only one species of plant; it can be difficult for pests and diseases to find their preferred hosts and establish a population in perennial beds, which often contain a mixture of different plant species. At the same time, because the plants are in the same spot for many years, pest problems can become permanent. The advantage is that the beneficial insects, birds and other pest-devouring organisms can also develop permanent populations.

For many years pest control meant spraying or dusting, with the goal to eliminate every pest in the landscape. A more moderate approach advocated today is known as IPM (Integrated Pest Management or Integrated Plant Management). The goal of IPM is to reduce pest problems to levels at which only negligible damage is done. Of course, you, the gardener, must determine what degree of damage is acceptable to you. Consider whether a pest's damage is localized or covers the entire plant. Will the damage being done kill the plant or is it only affecting the outward appearance? Are there methods of controlling the pest without chemicals?

Chemicals are the last resort, because they may do more harm than good. They endanger the gardener and his or her family and pets, and they kill as many good as bad organisms, leaving the whole garden vulnerable to even worse attacks. A good IPM program includes learning about your plants and what they need for healthy growth, what pests might affect your plants, where and when to look for those pests and how to control them. Keep records of pest damage because your observations can reveal patterns useful in spotting recurring problems and in planning your maintenance regime.

There are four steps in effective and responsible pest management. Cultural controls are the most important. Physical controls should be attempted next, followed by biological controls. Resort to chemical controls only when the first three possibilities have been exhausted.

Cultural controls are the gardening techniques you use in the daily care of your garden. Keeping your plants as healthy as possible is the best defense against pests. Growing perennials in the conditions they prefer and keeping your soil healthy, with plenty of organic matter, are just two of the cultural controls you

My favorite method of treating infected material is to place it into a black plastic bag and leave it in the hot sun for a week. The high heat kills microorganisms that would be dangerous. I then put it into the garbage that will be picked up and hauled away.

Snail eating a leaf (above); frogs eat many insect pests (below).

Coffee Grounds Spray
Boil 2 pounds used coffee grounds in 3 gallons water for about 10 minutes.
Allow to cool; strain the grounds out of the mixture. Apply as a spray.

can use to keep pests manageable. Choose resistant varieties of perennials that are not prone to problems. Space the plants so that they have good air circulation around them and are not stressed from competing for light, nutrients and space. Remove plants from the landscape if they are decimated by the same pests every year. Remove and burn or take to a permitted dump site diseased foliage and branches, and prevent the spread of disease by keeping your gardening tools clean and by tidying up fallen leaves and dead plant matter at the end of every growing season.

Physical controls are generally used to combat insect problems. An example of such a control is picking insects off plants by hand, which is not as daunting as it may seem if you catch the problem when it is just beginning. Large, slow insects are particularly easy to pick off. Other physical controls include barriers that stop insects from getting to the plant, and traps that catch or confuse insects. Physical control of diseases often necessitates removing the infected plant part or parts to prevent the spread of the problem.

Biological controls make use of populations of predators that prey on pests. Animals such as birds, snakes, frogs, spiders, lady beetles and certain bacteria can play an important role in keeping pest populations at a manageable level. Encourage these creatures to take up residence in your garden. A birdbath and birdfeeder will encourage birds to enjoy your yard and feed on a wide variety of insect pests. Many beneficial insects are probably already living in your landscape, and you can encourage them to stay by planting appropriate food sources. Many beneficial insects eat nectar from flowers such as yarrow.

Chemical controls should rarely be necessary, but if you must use them there are some 'organic' options available. Organic sprays are no less dangerous than chemical ones, but they will break down into harmless compounds. The main drawback to using any chemicals is that they may also kill the beneficial insects you have been trying to attract to your garden. Organic chemicals are available at most garden centers and you should follow the manufacturer's instructions carefully. A large amount of insecticide is not going to be any more effective in controlling pests than the recommended amount. Note that if a particular pest is not listed on the package, it will not be controlled by that product. Proper and early identification of pests is vital to finding a quick solution.

Whereas cultural, physical, biological and chemical controls are all possible defenses against insects, diseases can only be controlled culturally. It is most often weakened plants that succumb to diseases. Healthy plants can often fight off illness, although some diseases can infect plants regardless of their level of health. Prevention is often the only hope: once a plant has been infected, it should probably be destroyed, in order to prevent the disease from spreading.

Rule of thumb for mixing horticultural oil: 5 tablespoons oil per 1 gallon of water.

Recipes for ant control
Mix 3 cups of water, 1 cup of white sugar and 4 teaspoons of boric acid in a pot. (Boric acid is available in powdered or crystal form.) Bring this mix just to a boil and remove it from the heat source. Let the mix cool. Pour small amounts of this cooled mix into bottlecaps or other similar small containers and place them around the area you want to rid of ants. Another variation of this is to mix equal parts of Borax and icing sugar and apply in the same manner as above.

About This Guide

THE PERENNIALS IN THIS BOOK ARE ORGANIZED ALPHABETICALLY by their local common names. Additional common names and Latin names appear after the primary reference. Quick identification information on height, spread, hardiness, flower color and when to expect the plant to bloom are the first details given on each plant. The **Quick Reference Chart** at the back of the book will be a handy guide as you plan your garden.

For each entry, we describe our favorite recommended or alternate species, but keep in mind that many more hybrids, cultivars and varieties are often available. Check with your local greenhouses or garden centers when making your selection. The **Perennials at a Glance** section has one photo from each entry to allow you to become familiar with the different plants.

Pests or diseases common to a plant, if any, are listed for each entry. The section 'Problems & Pests' in the Introduction and the Glossary of Pests & Diseases at the back of the book provide information on how to solve the common problems that can plague your plants.

Because our region is so climatically diverse, we refer to the seasons in only the general sense. The zones map on p. 13 will help you determine the general growing conditions in your region.

Contra Costa County Library
Moraga
4/19/2023 4:51:50 PM

- Patron Receipt -
- Charges -

ID: 21901026612543

Item: 31901048319794
Title: Perennials for northern California /
Call Number: 635.932 TANEM
Due Date: 5/10/2023

Item: 31901068064700
Title: The kitchen garden /
Call Number: 635 BUCKINGHAM
Due Date: 5/10/2023

Account information, library hours,
and upcoming closures can be found
at https://ccclib.org/contact-us/,
or by calling 1-800-984-4636.

The Perennials

Anemone
Windflower
Anemone

Height: 6"–5' **Spread:** 6–24" **Flower color:** white, pink, red, blue
Blooms: spring, summer, fall **Hardiness:** hardy to semi-hardy

ANEMONES ARE COTTAGE-GARDEN PLANTS THAT WILL MAKE A wonderful addition to your flowerbeds. Although they can become invasive in some gardens, the invasiveness is easily controlled. Merely lift and divide plants each year and dispose of the excess roots. Add a lot of bulb food each time you divide and re-plant anemones in the fall. This treatment will increase the intensity of the blooms of *Anemone blanda*.

Planting

Seeding: Direct sow in autumn as soon as seeds are ripe

Transplanting: Fall, early spring

Spacing: 4–18"

Growing

Anemones prefer **partial or light shade.** *A.* x *hybrida* has fibrous, spreading roots and grows best in **humus-rich, moist** soil of **average to high fertility.** Divide *A.* x *hybrida* in early spring or fall or take root cuttings in spring.

A. blanda and *A.* x *fulgens* have tuberous roots and prefer a **light, fertile, well-drained, moist** soil when growing and flowering and a dry soil while dormant. Divide the tubers of *A. blanda* and *A.* x *fulgens* in summer when the plants are dormant. Plant tubers 1–2" deep and ensure they are properly oriented in the ground. The old stem will leave a depressed scar on the tuber. Make sure the scarred side is facing up. *A. blanda* is often planted in the fall with other spring-blooming plants such as tulips. Although these plants will naturalize and not require water after the first year, they will perform much better with regular garden watering. The tubers can be left in the flowerbeds for bloom the next year.

Tips

Anemones make beautiful additions to lightly shaded beds, borders and woodland gardens. They are a great choice for providing late-season flowers. They will multiply on their own and spread to other parts of

A. x *hybrida* (this page)

The name Anemone *comes from the Greek* anemos, 'wind,' *a reference to the windswept habitats of many species.*

your garden. The long stems make good cut flowers.

Grecian Windflower and Scarlet Windflower are effective when used in rock gardens, beds, borders, woodlands and in containers.

Apply mulch in fall in areas that experience prolonged, deep cold.

Recommended

A. blanda (Grecian Windflower) is a low, spreading, tuberous perennial 6–8" tall, with an equal spread. It bears blue flowers in spring. **'White Splendor'** is a vigorous plant with white flowers.

A. x *fulgens* (Scarlet Windflower) grows 12" tall and 6" wide. Scarlet flowers with dark violet to black stamens bloom in spring. Scarlet Windflower can handle some moisture when dormant (after flowering).

A. x *hybrida* (Japanese Anemone) is an upright, suckering perennial

A. blanda 'White Splendor' (above),
A. x *hybrida* cultivar (below)

24–60" tall and about 24" wide. It bears intense pink, red or white flowers from late summer to mid-fall. There are numerous cultivars available. '**Honorine Jobert**' has plentiful white flowers. '**Max Vogel**' has large pink flowers. '**Pamina**' has pinkish red double flowers. '**Prince Henry**' is shorter than most cultivars, with flowers of deep rose pink. '**Whirlwind**' has semi-double white flowers with twisted green tepals at the flower center. Most of the plants sold as *A. japonica* are actually *A.* x *hybrida*.

Problems & Pests

Rare, but possible, problems include leaf gall, downy mildew, powdery mildew, smut, fungal leaf spot, rust, nematodes, caterpillars, slugs and flea beetles. Watch for migrating sparrows in early spring as the plants begin to sprout.

A. x *hybrida* (this page)

Aster

Aster

Height: 10"–5' **Spread:** 18"–4' **Flower color:** red, white, blue, purple, pink
Blooms: early summer to mid-fall **Hardiness:** hardy to semi-hardy

IF YOU ARE INTERESTED IN A CAREFREE ADDITION TO YOUR old-fashioned garden, asters are the plants for you. If you live in an area with lots of snow, asters, along with beard tongue plants, can form the foundation of your garden. Although asters benefit from biannual division, they forgive neglect and will bloom for years. They are a favorite when nothing else is blooming.

Planting

Seeding: Not recommended

Transplanting: March through September; from one-gallon containers

Spacing: 18–36"

Growing

Asters prefer **full sun** but tolerate partial shade. The soil should be **fertile, moist** and **well drained.** Pinch or shear these plants back in early summer to promote dense growth and reduce disease problems.

Divide every one to two years in early spring or late fall to maintain vigor, control spread and to increase the number of plants if desired.

Tips

Asters can be used in the middle or back of borders and in cottage gardens. They can also be naturalized in wild gardens.

A. novi-belgii

Aster is Latin for 'star,' and these plants were once called starworts because of the many petals that radiate from the center.

'Purple Dome' (bottom left) with *A. novi-belgii* (upper right)

Recommended

A. x *frikartii* bears light to dark purple flowers nonstop and abundantly from early summer to fall. These hybrids like a well-drained spot and can be temperamental. They may need re-planting after several years. They grow up to 24" and spread 18–24". 'Mönch' is a taller variety, up to 30", with abundant lavender blue flowers.

A. novae-angliae (Michaelmas Daisy, New England Aster) is an upright, spreading, clump-forming perennial. It grows to 3–5' tall and spreads 24"–4'. From late summer to mid-fall it bears yellow-centered purple flowers. 'Alma Potschke' bears bright salmon pink or cherry red flowers. It grows 36–48" tall and spreads 24". 'Purple Dome' is dwarf and spreading with dark purple flowers. This cultivar is mildew resistant. It grows 18–24" tall and spreads 24–30".

A. novae-angliae (above), *A. novi-belgii* (below)

A. novi-belgii (Michaelmas Daisy, New York Aster) is a dense, upright, clump-forming perennial. It grows 3–4' tall and spreads 18–36". '**Alice Haslam**' is a dwarf plant with bright pink flowers. It grows 10–18" tall and spreads 18". '**Chequers**' is a compact plant with purple flowers. '**Persian Rose**' is also compact, growing 12" tall and 18" wide, and bears rose pink flowers.

Problems & Pests

Possible problems include powdery mildew, aster wilt, aster yellows, aphids, mites, slugs and snails.

What looks like a single flower on asters and other daisy-like plants is actually a cluster of many flowers. Look closely at the center of the flowerhead and you will see all the tiny individual flowers.

A. novae-angliae (above), *A. novi-belgii* (below)

Astilbe

Astilbe

Height: 1–5' **Spread:** 8–36" **Flower color:** white, pink, purple, peach, red
Blooms: early, mid- or late summer **Hardiness:** hardy

ASTILBES ARE PERFECT FOR WET, SHADY SPOTS IN THE GARDEN.
When I was very young, my grandparents' home in Northern California was at
the base of a slight slope and thus had all the water from the hillside. Astilbes
were ideal for these moist conditions. When I picked the astilbe blooms I could
tickle my cousin Bob with them when he took off his shirt on a hot day. This
did not make Grandma happy if she caught me, but her mild reprimand did
not prevent me from what I thought was one of life's pleasures.

Astilbes make lovely cut flowers,
and if you leave the plumes in
a vase as the water evaporates,
you'll have dried flowers to enjoy
all winter.

Planting

Seeding: Not recommended; seedlings do not come true to type

Transplanting: Spring

Spacing: 10" for *A. arendsii*; 24–36" for *A. chinensis*

Growing

Astilbes prefer **light or partial shade** and tolerate full shade, though with reduced flowering. The soil should be **fertile, humus rich, acidic, moist** and **well drained**. These plants like to grow near water sources, such as ponds and streams, but they dislike standing in water. Provide a mulch in summer to keep the roots cool and moist. Divide every three years in spring or fall to maintain plant vigor.

Astilbe flowers fade to various shades of brown. They may be removed once flowering is finished, or they may be left in place. The flowerheads look interesting and natural in the garden well into fall.

A. x *arendsii* (this page)

A. x arendsii (above & next page)

These plants self-seed easily but self-seeded plants are unlikely to look like the parent plant.

Tips

Grow astilbes near the edge of bog gardens or ponds and in woodland gardens and shaded borders. Astilbes tend to be short-lived in the Central Valley.

The root crown tends to lift out of the soil as the plant grows bigger. This problem can be solved by applying a top dressing of rich soil as a mulch when the plant starts lifting or by re-planting the entire plant deeper into the soil.

Recommended

A. x *arendsii* (Astilbe, False Spirea) grows 18–48" tall and spreads 18–36". Many cultivars are available from this hybrid group. The following are a few popular ones. 'Amethyst' bears lavender flowers in late summer to early fall on plants 4' tall. '**Bressingham Beauty**' grows to 36" tall and 24" wide and bears bright pink flowers in mid-summer. '**Deutschland**' grows 20" tall and spreads 12". It bears white flowers in late spring. '**Fanal**' reaches 30" in height. It bears red flowers in early summer and has deep bronze foliage. '**Peach Blossom**' grows about 20" tall and bears peach-pink flowers in early summer.

Alternate Species

A. chinensis (Chinese Astilbe) is a dense, vigorous perennial that tolerates dry soil better than other astilbe species. It grows about 24" tall and spreads 18". It bears fluffy white, pink or purple flowers in late summer. **Var.** *pumila* is more commonly available than the species. This plant forms a low groundcover with dark pink flowers. It grows 10–15" tall and spreads 8–10". **Var.** *taquetti* 'Superba' is a tall form, growing to 5', with vivid lavender purple flowers produced in a long narrow spike.

Problems & Pests

A variety of pests, including aphids, can occasionally attack astilbes. Powdery mildew, bacterial leaf spot and fungal leaf spot are also possible problems.

With their fern-like foliage and showy plume flowers, astilbes are favorite summer flowering perennials.

In late summer, transplant seedlings found near the parent plant for plumes of color throughout the garden.

Baby's Breath

Gypsophila

Height: 8"–4' **Spread:** 12"–4' **Flower color:** white, pink
Blooms: most of summer **Hardiness:** hardy

I HAVE USED BABY'S BREATH SPECIES IN A PICKING GARDEN ALONG
with marigolds, Transvaal Daisy and other picking perennials and annuals.
Baby's breath plants are wonderful in any flower arrangement. In the garden
the plants create an open, airy effect and contrast well with plants that bear
large flowers and foliage. Mulching established plants will ensure their early
growth in the spring.

Planting

Seeding: Sow in containers in cold frame in spring; some varieties cannot be grown from seed

Transplanting: Year-round from one-gallon containers; spring for cooler areas above 3000' altitude

Spacing: 36"; small varieties may be planted closer together

Growing

Grow these plants in a location with **full sun.** The soil must be **neutral or alkaline,** of **average fertility** and very **well drained.** In moist, acidic soil these plants are prone to rotting. The low-growing varieties can withstand more moisture than the larger types and are better for coastal gardens.

G. repens (this page)

Fresh or dried, baby's breath flowers make a wonderful addition to arrangements.

Some cultivars are grafted onto stronger rootstock. When planting these cultivars, it is important to plant so that the graft union—a fat knob where the two plants are joined—is about an inch below the soil surface, to help the plant above the graft grow its own roots.

Baby's breath plants develop a large, thick taproot that should not be disturbed once it is established, so do not divide these plants. Rather, propagate them by root cuttings in late winter or by basal cuttings in summer.

Tips

Baby's breath plants, with their cloud-like flower clusters, tie together other plantings in a border. They are effective when planted with plants that have broad leaves.

To prolong the flowering period, it is best to deadhead baby's breath. This task sounds easy enough until the plants are covered in tiny blooms, all in different stages of development. Instead of trying to take off those flowers that have faded, wait until the plants are almost finished flowering and then shear them back lightly. This technique will encourage new growth and a second flush of blooms later in the season.

Recommended

G. paniculata is a mound-forming, open, branched perennial. It grows 3–4' tall and wide and bears white or pink flowers for an extended period in summer. '**Bristol Fairy**' grows to 4' tall and wide and bears pure white, double flowers. '**Perfecta**' has large, white, double flowers and also grows 4' tall and wide. '**Pink Star**' has pink double flowers. It grows up to 18" tall. '**Rosy Veil**' is a mound-forming hybrid with pink double

G. paniculata with *Lychnis coronaria* and other perennials

flowers. It grows about 16–20" tall and up to 36" wide. **'Viette's Dwarf'** is a smaller plant, 12–16" tall, with pink double flowers.

Alternate Species

G. repens is a low-growing species. It grows up to 8" tall and spreads to form a mat 12–20" wide. This species is more acid tolerant than *G. paniculata* and may be used in rock gardens, on rock walls, on pathway edges or to edge a border.

Problems & Pests

Baby's breath plants attract slugs. Problems with crown gall, bacterial soft rot or crown or stem rot can be avoided if the drainage has been improved with organic matter such as alfalfa pellets.

'Rosy Veil' (above), *G. paniculata* (below)

Balloon Flower

Platycodon

Height: 24–36" **Spread:** 18–24" **Flower color:** blue, pink, white
Blooms: summer to mid-fall **Hardiness:** hardy

IF YOU ARE EVER FEELING TENSE, GO AHEAD AND POP A COUPLE
of the blooms of Balloon Flower. Just don't let the kids see—if they discover
that the flower buds pop when squeezed, you won't have a lot of flowers left!
Balloon Flower is a vigorous perennial that will last for years without being
disturbed. The purplish blue flowers add a cool color to the summer garden.
Balloon Flower is at its blooming best July through October.

Planting

Seeding: Indoors in late winter or direct sow in spring; blooms second year after seeding

Transplanting: Mid-March through June; from six-packs or 4" pots

Spacing: 12–18"

Growing

Balloon Flower grows well in **full sun** or **partial shade**. The soil should be of **average to rich fertility, light, moist** and **well drained.** This plant dislikes wet soil. It sprouts late in the year, so mark its location to avoid accidentally damaging it before it sprouts.

When transplanting Balloon Flower into your garden, use a light touch loosening the root ball. If the plants are hopelessly root-bound, return them to where you purchased them.

Balloon Flower rarely needs dividing. It resents having its roots disturbed and can take a long time to re-establish after dividing. Propagate by gently detaching the side shoots that sprout up around the plant. Plants will self-seed and the seedlings can be moved to new locations.

Tips

Use Balloon Flower in borders, rock gardens and cottage gardens.

Pinch off spent flowers to improve appearance and extend the blooming period. Remove just the spent flower, not the entire stem.

Recommended

P. grandiflorus is an upright, clump-forming perennial; the cultivars tend to be lower and more rounded. **Var.** *albus* bears white flowers, often veined with blue. **'Double Blue'** is a compact plant with purple-blue double flowers. **'Fuji Blue'** from Japan has deep blue flowers, excellent for cutting. **'Fuji Pink'** bears clear pink flowers. **'Sentimental Blue'** is a new dwarf form with intense blue flowers, good for containers.

Problems & Pests

Potential problems include slugs, snails and occasionally leaf spot or blight. Gophers can also be a problem.

'Double Blue' (below)

Basket-of-Gold
Aurinia

Height: 3–12" **Spread:** 8–18" **Flower color:** yellow, apricot
Blooms: late winter to late spring **Hardiness:** hardy

THE OUTSTANDING COLOR OF BASKET-OF-GOLD BLOOMS WILL add a wonderful golden hue to gardens that look sad in winter and early spring. When you combine the bloom color with the gray foliage, you have a plant that can accent just about any of your favorite perennials. Basket-of-gold can be used as an evergreen addition to moss baskets, and it is a great plant to combine with dark red geraniums.

Planting

Seeding: Sow seeds in containers in cold frame in spring

Transplanting: Early to mid-spring

Spacing: 8–18"

Growing

Basket-of-gold prefers **full sun** but tolerates partial to light shade. The soil should be of **average to poor fertility, sandy** and **well drained.** Basket-of-gold can rot in wet soil, and growth becomes floppy in rich soil. It is drought tolerant once established.

Shearing the entire plant back by about half after flowering will rejuvenate the foliage. Shearing it back lightly after each bloom cycle will keep the plant compact and encourage more flowers. Do not shear off all flowerheads in hot regions, because the plants do not live as long when exposed to high temperatures. Self-seeding will provide new plants once the old ones die.

Do not move or divide established plants. Propagate by cuttings taken from the new growth that emerges after flowering.

Tips

Use in borders and rock gardens, along wall tops and as a groundcover in difficult or little-used areas.

Avoid planting Basket-of-gold near slow-growing plants because it can quickly choke them out.

Recommended

A. saxatilis is a vigorous, mound-forming perennial. It grows 8–12"

tall, 12–18" wide and bears bright yellow flowers. '**Citrina**' bears light lemon yellow flowers. '**Compacta**' bears golden yellow flowers. It is a bit smaller than the species, growing about 6" tall and 8" wide. '**Dudley Nevill**' bears apricot-colored flowers. '**Gold Ball**' is a clump-forming plant up to 6" tall with bright yellow flowers held above the foliage. '**Tom Thumb**' is a very low grower, reaching a height of 3". Its flowers and leaves are also small. '**Variegata**' bears lemon yellow flowers and has irregular cream-colored margins on the foliage.

Bear's Breeches
Acanthus

Height: 3–5' **Spread:** 3–4' **Flower color:** purple, rose purple, white
Blooms: late spring to mid-summer **Hardiness:** hardy

BEAR'S BREECHES WERE AMONG THE FIRST PLANTS I PUT INTO MY
garden before I became a nurseryman. They are great tropical-looking
plants. In the cool coastal areas these plants can take off, even becoming
invasive, and they tolerate the bog conditions found on the coast of Northern California. Great companion plants are other large-leaved summer
plants such as ginger and banana palm.

Planting

Seeding: Start seeds in containers in spring

Transplanting: Any time

Spacing: 36"

Growing

Bear's breeches will grow in **full sun** to **full shade** in just about any **well-drained** soil. They prefer a **rich, moist** soil, but you may wish to plant in a slightly poorer soil to keep them from being too aggressive. Be sure to keep the plants well watered if planted during hot, dry weather to help them become established. They are drought tolerant but will do best if given an occasional soaking when the weather is hot and dry. Bear's breeches dislike overly humid conditions.

These plants die all the way back in the summer after blooming. They leaf out again in November after the rains have begun. They tolerate frost in our area down to 15° F.

Acanthus is derived from the Greek akanthos ('thorny'), a reference to the often spiny nature of these plants. It is one of the oldest named perennials.

A. spinosus (this page)

Bear's breeches may require frequent division. Divisions should be made from late fall to early spring. These plants grow best from root cuttings.

Tips

Bear's breeches are bold and dramatic plants that form large clumps. They work well as the central planting in an island bed or at the back of a border. The foliage is almost as striking as the flower stalks.

Invasiveness is the single most important thing to keep in mind when dealing with bear's breeches. The plants spread by rhizomes and even a small piece left in the ground may start a new plant. Provide natural or artificial barriers to a minimum depth of 8", or plant bear's breeches where they have plenty of space to grow.

A. mollis (above), *A. spinosus* (below)

Recommended

A. mollis (Common Bear's Breeches) forms a large clump of lobed foliage. It is less spiny than *A. spinosus*. Tall spikes of white-and-purple bicolored flowers are borne in late spring to summer.

A. spinosus (Spiny Bear's Breeches) forms a clump of silvery, very spiny foliage. It is more tolerant of humid conditions and winter cold and is less invasive than *A. mollis*. The white flowers with purple to rose-purple bracts are borne from early spring to mid-summer.

A. spinosus

Problems & Pests

These plants may have trouble with snails, slugs, powdery mildew and leaf spot. Good ventilation prevents fungal problems. If a plant does get powdery mildew, it is usually when it is going into its resting period, which lasts about six weeks. Remove the old leaves to prevent any mildew from spreading to the new leaves.

The foliage of A. spinosus *was imitated by the Greeks as a pattern to decorate their architecture. This is especially evident in the Corinthian Order of Greek architecture.*

Beard Tongue
Penstemon
Penstemon

Height: 12"–4' **Spread:** 12–36" **Flower color:** pink, purple, red, coral, blue
Blooms: spring, summer **Hardiness:** hardy

BEARD TONGUE PLANTS ADD HEIGHT AND LONG-LASTING COLOR
to any perennial or cottage garden. These plants are perfect additions to butterfly and hummingbird gardens. Combine with Mexican Sage, Pineapple
Sage and Gaura for an open invitation to all of these friends of the garden.
Border Penstemon is a favorite of Sierra gardeners because of its hardiness
and long blooming period.

Planting

Seeding: Sow seeds in late winter or spring; soil temperature 55–64° F

Transplanting: Spring or fall

Spacing: About 12"

Growing

Beard tongue plants prefer **full sun** or **partial shade**. The soil should be very **well drained** and **fertile** for *P.* x *gloxinoides* but of **poor to average fertility** for *P. heterophyllus*. Beard tongues tolerate drought.

Pinch plants when they are 12" tall to encourage bushy growth. Divide every two or three years in spring.

Tips

The flowers of beard tongue plants work well in a mixed border, cottage garden or rock garden. To support the tall stems, insert twiggy branches around the plants in spring before they grow tall and floppy.

About 250 species of Penstemon *grow in varied habitats from mountains to open plains throughout North and South America.*

These plants tend to be short-lived. On occasion the plants will die for no apparent reason. Taking cuttings in summer and fall will help avoid the disappointment of having your favorite beard tongue die.

Recommended

P. x *gloxinoides* (Border Penstemon) is a group of upright hybrids with loose clusters of large, white-throated flowers in shades of pink and red. The flowers bloom on and off all summer and into November. 'Alice Hindley' grows 3–4' tall, spreads 18–24" and produces white-throated, pale mauve flowers. '**Apple Blossom**' grows 18–24" tall and wide and has pale pink flowers with white throats. '**Evelyn**' grows 18–30" tall and 12–15" wide. The rose pink flowers are slightly lighter on the inside than the outside, and the insides are marked with dark pink lines. '**Kissed**' series grows 24–28" tall and spreads up to 36". The flowers have white throats and come in shades of red, coral and purple. '**Midnight**' grows 18–36" tall and up to 18" wide. The flowers come in dark purple to indigo blue with white throats. '**Rubicundus**' grows 3–4' tall and 18" wide and bears red flowers with white throats.

P. heterophyllus (Foothills Pensте-mon) grows 12–24" tall and wide. Light pink-purple flowers bloom in spring to early summer. **Var.** *purdyi* (subsp. *purdyi*) (California Blue Bedder) is a mat-forming plant growing 18–24" tall and 24–36" wide. It bears sky blue to deep blue flowers in summer.

Problems & Pests

Powdery mildew, rust and leaf spot may be problems. Water in the early morning only to help avoid diseases. Slugs and snails may damage young foliage. To protect against these pests, use a slug bait, such as Sluggo™.

The flowers attract butterflies and hummingbirds in the summer.

'Midnight' (above)

Bee Balm
Bergamot
Monarda

Height: 24"–4' **Spread:** 12–24" **Flower color:** red, pink **Blooms:** summer
Hardiness: hardy

THE REWARDS OF BEE BALM WELL OFFSET ITS TENDENCY TO
spread. It attracts bees so should not be planted near heavy foot traffic areas.
My daughter Edie is allergic to bee stings and was once stung by a bee. After
that happened, I introduced Edie to a bee. I told her she had a choice. She
could be afraid of the bee, at which time the bee would sting, or she could
ignore the bee, at which time the bee would ignore her. She chose to ignore
the bee and hasn't had another bee sting since.
She continues to enjoy gardening while
ignoring the bees and even has some
Bee Balm growing in her garden.

*The other common name,
Bergamot, comes from the
scent of the Italian Bergamot
orange (*Citrus bergamia*),
often used in aromatherapy.*

Planting

Seeding: Sow seeds in containers in cold frame in spring or fall

Transplanting: Any time; March is best

Spacing: 18–24"

Growing

Bee Balm will do equally well in **full sun** or **partial shade**. The soil should be of **average fertility, humus rich, moist** and **well drained.**

Divide every two or three years in spring before the new growth emerges, and prune back low to the ground every spring.

Tips

Use Bee Balm along a stream or pond or in the dappled shade of a woodland border. It may be used in a well-watered border.

This plant's scientific name honors the Spanish botanist and physician Nicholas Monardes (1493–1588).

Bee Balm will attract bees, butter-flies and hummingbirds. Avoid using pesticides that can seriously harm or kill these creatures, especially if you plan to ingest this, or any plant, in your garden.

The fresh or dried leaves may be used to make a refreshing, minty citrus tea. Put a handful of fresh leaves in a teapot, pour boiling water over the leaves and let steep for at least five minutes. Sweeten the tea with honey to suit your own taste.

Recommended

M. didyma is a bushy, mounding plant that forms a thick clump of stems. Red or pink flowers are borne in late summer. '**Cambridge Scarlet**' bears flowers in bright scarlet red. '**Gardenview Scarlet**' bears large red flowers and is resistant to powdery

mildew. **'Marshall's Delight'** doesn't come true to type from seed and must be propagated by cuttings or divisions. It is very resistant to powdery mildew and bears pink flowers. **'Panorama'** is a group of hybrids with flowers in scarlet, pink or salmon. **'Raspberry Wine'** bears red blooms on dark green foliage. This cultivar is an excellent choice for cut flowers.

Problems & Pests

Powdery mildew is the worst problem, but rust and leaf spot can cause trouble. To help prevent powdery mildew, thin the stems in spring. If the plant is afflicted with mildew after flowering, cut the plant back to 6" to increase air circulation.

'Marshall's Delight' (above)

Bellflower

Campanula

Height: 2–18" **Spread:** 6–36" **Flower color:** blue, white, purple, pink
Blooms: spring, summer **Hardiness:** hardy

BEAUTIFUL BELLFLOWERS HAVE SO MANY USES. I HAVE USED THE deer-resistant *C. isophylla* as a groundcover under a Southern Magnolia. Its delicate foliage and white flowers are delightful, and the blue-flowering varieties can provide the same type of cover. In the hot valleys, mulching through the summer is important.

Planting

Seeding: Direct sow in spring to early summer; germination can be erratic

Transplanting: Spring; best from six-packs

Spacing: 12–36"

Growing

Bellflowers grow well in **full sun, partial shade** or **light shade**. The soil should be of **average to high fertility** and **well drained**. Ensure you provide adequate water. Bellflower plants appreciate summer mulch to keep their roots cool.

Amending the soil with organic matter such as compost or alfalfa pellets and ensuring good drainage are two important things you can do to ensure success with any bellflower plant.

Bellflowers respond well to deadheading to prolong blooming. Use scissors to cut back one-third of the plant at a time. As the pruned section starts to bud, cut back other sections.

It is important to divide bellflowers every few years in early spring or fall to keep plants vigorous and to prevent them from becoming invasive.

Tips

Low, spreading and trailing bellflowers can be used in rock gardens, on rock walls and to edge beds. Upright and mounding bellflowers can be used in borders and cottage gardens.

Some varieties are available as mature plants in one-gallon containers in summer. These will be in bloom and make a show immediately in the garden.

C. rotundifolia goes well with perennials such as Balloon Flower and *Limonium latifolium* (Sea Lavender).

Bellflower plants can be propagated by basal, new-growth or rhizome cuttings.

C. rotundifolia (below)

C. isophylla (above), *C. poscharskyana* (below)

There are over 300 species of Campanula *found throughout the Northern Hemisphere in habitats ranging from high rocky crags to boggy meadows.*

Recommended

C. carpatica (Carpathian Bellflower, Carpathian Harebell) is a spreading, mounding perennial. The clumps of foliage grow 4–8" tall and spread 8–20" wide. The blue, white or purple flowers are borne on 8–12" tall stems in summer. '**Blue Clips**' and '**White Clips**' are smaller, compact plants with large blue or white flowers '**Jewel**' is low growing, 4–8" tall, and has deep blue flowers. '**Kent Belle**' is a stately new hybrid with large, deep violet-blue bells on arching stems.

C. isophylla (Italian Bellflower, Star of Bethlehem, Falling Stars) grows 6–8" tall and trails to 24". Pale blue to white flowers are produced for a long period in late summer to fall. '**Alba**' has larger, pure white flowers. **Kristal Hybrids** are compact, vigorous plants with larger blooms than the species. They are good choices for hanging baskets and containers. Of these hybrids, '**Stella Blue**' has bright purple-blue blooms and '**Stella White**' bears white blooms.

C. poscharskyana (Serbian Bellflower) is a trailing perennial that grows 6–12" tall and 24–36" wide. It bears light purple flowers in spring to early summer. Plant it in shade in the hot interior valleys. It grows well near pools and makes a flowery groundcover around shade-loving shrubs such as fuchsias and hydrangeas. This species doesn't need as much water as the others.

C. rotundifolia (Harebell, Scottish Bluebell) is a trailing or clump-forming perennial. The foliage grows 2–5" tall and the flowering stems 6–18" tall. The plant spreads 6–12" and produces clusters of bright blue to white flowers in summer. **'Olympica'** has larger flowers and darker green, toothed foliage.

Problems & Pests

Watch for slugs and snails. Problems with vine weevils, spider mites, aphids, powdery mildew, rust and fungal leaf spot are possible.

'White Clips' (above), *C. carpatica* (below)

Bergenia

Bergenia

Height: 12–24" **Spread:** 18–24" **Flower color:** red, purple, pink
Blooms: early spring **Hardiness:** hardy

I HAVE ALWAYS BEEN IMPRESSED WITH BERGENIAS ALONG SOME
of the older landscapes in my area. Here they are next to the sidewalk, with
the soil being compacted by foot traffic, and still they bloom magnificently
in January and February in a downpour of rain. The tropical foliage seems to
stay green even in this neglected situation. In some of the finer estates they
are used as an evergreen border plant with complementary plantings of
summer annuals.

*Bergenias are called evergreen
perennials. The foliage is actually
a reddish color in winter, when
the plant draws moisture from
the leaves.*

Planting

Seeding: Fresh, ripe seeds should be sown uncovered; indoors in late winter or early spring, outdoors when soil temperature is 69–70° F

Transplanting: Spring

Spacing: 18"

Growing

Bergenias grow well in **partial to full shade**. Plant in **full shade** in the hot interior valleys. The soil should be of **average to rich fertility, well drained** and preferably **moist**.

Propagating by seed can be somewhat risky. You may not get what you hoped for. A more certain way to get more of the plants you have is to propagate them with root cuttings. Bergenias spread just below the surface by rhizomes, which may be cut off in pieces and grown separately as long as a leaf shoot is attached to the section.

B. cordifolia (this page)

Bergenias make nice feature plants in spring. After flowering is complete, the leathery leaves help cover the bare spots left by spring-flowering bulbs, adding bulk and substance to the garden all season.

B. cordifolia (this page)

Divide every two to three years in late winter to early spring when the clump begins to die out in the middle. You can cut back the foliage annually if the plant looks leggy. Once established, bergenias are low maintenance.

Tips

These versatile, low-growing, spreading plants can be used as groundcovers, to edge borders and pathways, in rock gardens and under trees and shrubs.

Once flowering is complete, bergenias still look beautiful with their thick, leathery, glossy leaves. These plants are a soothing background for other flowers because of their expanse of green. As well, many varieties turn attractive colors of bronze and purple in fall and winter.

Recommended

B. cordifolia (Heart-leaved Bergenia) grows to 24" tall with an equal or greater spread. Its pink flowers bloom in summer. The foliage turns bronze or purple in fall and winter. 'Purpurea' has magenta-purple flowers and red-tinged foliage.

B. crassifolia (Siberian Tea, Leather Bergenia, Winter-blooming Bergenia) grows 12–18" tall and 18" wide. The light pink-purple, nodding flowers bloom in late winter to early spring.

B. **'Evening Glow'** ('Abendglut')
grows about 12" tall and spreads
18–24". The flowers are a deep
magenta-crimson. The foliage turns
red and maroon in winter.

Problems & Pests

Bergenias may have problems with
slugs and snails and, infrequently,
fungal leaf spot, root rot, weevils,
caterpillars and foliar nematodes.

*These plants are also known as
elephant ears because of their
large, leathery leaves.*

Bidens
Bidens

Height: 12–36" **Spread:** 12–36" or more **Flower color:** yellow
Blooms: late spring to fall **Hardiness:** semi-hardy

ON MY MORNING RUN I PASS A FIELD OF NATIVE PLANTS THAT includes Bidens. This colorful plant creates a floating cloud of yellow blooms. The only problem with it is that the seeds get caught on my running shoes. Bidens in the garden provides the same wonderful effect, including the barbed seeds that stick to your shoes and clothes. This is the perfect perennial to plant on a clay hillside along with other native flowering plants.

Planting

Seeding: Indoors in late winter or direct sow in late spring

Transplanting: After last frost

Spacing: 12–24"

Growing

Bidens grows well in **full sun**. The soil should be **average to fertile, moist** and **well drained**. Ensure you provide plenty of water for the best performance, especially in the hottest weather.

If Bidens plants become lanky or unruly or overgrow their boundaries, cut them back to encourage new growth and fall flowers.

Tips

Bidens can be included in mixed borders, containers, hanging baskets and window boxes. Its fine foliage and bright flowers make it a useful filler between other plants.

Recommended

B. ferulifolia is a bushy, mounding or trailing plant with fine, fern-like foliage. It grows 24–36" tall, with an equal or greater spread. It bears bright yellow flowers for an extended period. **'Golden Eye'** is a compact plant growing 12" tall and wide. **'Golden Goddess'** grows 18–24" and has narrower foliage and larger flowers than the species.

Problems & Pests

Fungal problems such as leaf spot, powdery mildew and rust are possible. If your plant suffers fungal problems, cut it back to three inches; it will grow back without the problem as summer heat takes over.

Bidens is derived from the Latin and means 'two-toothed,' referring to the two barbs on each seed.

B. ferulifolia with Million Bells (below)

Black-Eyed Susan
Orange Cone Flower
Rudbeckia

Height: 18"–6' **Spread:** 12–36" **Flower color:** yellow, orange; brown or green centers **Blooms:** mid-summer to fall **Hardiness:** hardy

BLACK-EYED SUSANS ARE EASY TO GROW AND BRING MY FAVORITE color, yellow, into the garden. Yellow is a great color because it is works well with other perennials and cheers you up on a cloudy or foggy day. The impressive, tall-blooming *R. nitida* adds an accent to any landscape. Combining this plant with Pineapple Sage, Cleveland Sage, and other tall perennials will color the garden and attract butterflies as well as hummingbirds. For large swaths of yellow, *R. fulgida* is preferred.

Planting

Seeding: Indoors in early spring or outdoors in a cold frame; soil temperature 61–64° F

Transplanting: Spring

Spacing: 12–36"

Growing

Black-eyed Susans grow well in **full sun** and can take partial shade. The soil should be of **average fertility** and **well drained**. A fairly heavy clay soil is preferred. Regular watering is best, but established plants are drought tolerant.

These tough, long-lived perennials require very little maintenance. Divide in spring or fall every three to five years. Pinch plants in late spring to make bushier stands.

Tips

Plant black-eyed Susans in masses in a wildflower or naturalistic garden, in borders and in cottage-style gardens.

Black-eyed Susans spread by rhizomes, *R. fulgida* slowly, and *R. nitida* more aggressively.

Recommended

R. fulgida is an upright plant growing 18–36" tall and 12–24" wide. The orange-yellow flowers have brown centers. **Var.** *sullivantii* **'Goldsturm'** is more commonly available than the species. It bears large, bright yellow flowers.

R. fulgida (this page), with *Echinacea* (below)

R. nitida is an upright, spreading plant. It grows 3–6' tall and spreads 24–36". The yellow flowers have green centers. **'Autumn Glory'** has golden yellow flowers. **'Herbstsonne'** ('Autumn Sun') has bright yellow flowers on tall, sturdy stems. The seedheads attract birds.

Problems & Pests

Slugs and snails may attack young plants. Problems with aphids, rust, smut and leaf spot are possible. These plants are deer resistant.

Bleeding Heart
Dicentra

Height: 18–36" **Spread:** 18–36" **Flower color:** pink, white
Blooms: spring, summer **Hardiness:** hardy

WHEN BACKPACKING IN THE HIGH SIERRA, I WAS ONCE MET WITH the spectacular sight of bleeding heart plants along the streambanks. They bloom there from the first of April all through summer. In the home garden these effects are hard to match, and the plants may not survive the heat of summer. They are a wonderful accent in a fern garden. Both Western Bleeding Heart and Common Bleeding Heart can be evergreen all year in cool areas, but in the hot Central Valley they will disappear with the summer heat. In coastal areas they are short-lived and will need to be re-planted every two or three years.

Planting

Seeding: Start freshly ripened seed in a cold frame. Plants self-seed in the garden.

Transplanting: Early spring from bareroot stock; April through June from one-gallon containers

Spacing: 18–36"

Growing

Bleeding hearts prefer **light shade** but tolerate full sun or full shade. The soil should be **moist, light, well drained** and **humus rich**. Though these plants prefer to remain evenly moist, they are drought tolerant, particularly if the weather doesn't get hot. Very dry summer conditions will cause the plant to die back, but it will revive in fall or the following spring. Constant moisture will keep the flowers coming until mid-summer.

Common Bleeding Heart rarely needs dividing. Western Bleeding Heart can be divided every three years or so.

D. formosa (above), *D. spectabilis* (below)

D. formosa and D. spectabilis hybridize freely. If you grow both in your garden you may get interesting new hybrid seedlings popping up.

Use a lot of bulb food and peat moss or leaf mold when you plant bleeding hearts.

Tips

Bleeding hearts are versatile plants that look good in many places. The fern-like foliage and tiny, pendulous flowers make this plant desirable for woodland or shade gardens where they can be left to naturalize. They also work well in a mixed border or as early-season specimen plants. Try them near a pond or stream or in a large rock garden.

Recommended

D. formosa (Western Bleeding Heart) is a low-growing, wide-spreading plant about 18" tall and 24–36" wide. The pink flowers fade to white as they mature. This plant is likely to self-seed. It also spreads by

D. formosa (above), *D. spectabilis* 'Alba' (below)

rhizomes and can become invasive.
Var. *alba* has white flowers.

D. spectabilis (Common Bleeding
Heart) forms a large, elegant
mound. It grows 24–36" tall and
spreads about 18–36". The inner
petals are white and the outer petals
are pink. This species is likely to die
back in the summer heat and
prefers light dappled shade. 'Alba'
has entirely white flowers.

Problems & Pests

Slugs, downy mildew, *Verticillium*
wilt, viruses, rust and fungal leaf
spot can cause occasional problems.

*These delicate plants are the
perfect addition to the moist
woodland garden. Plant them
next to a shaded pond or stream.*

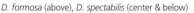

D. formosa (above), *D. spectabilis* (center & below)

Blue Eyes
Brunnera

Height: 18" **Spread:** 20–24" **Flower color:** blue **Blooms:** spring to early summer **Hardiness:** hardy

BLUE EYES IS A GREAT BULB COVER AND ACCENTS THE COLOR OF such spring-blooming plants as Forsythia and other deciduous shrubbery. Most nurseries will not carry this plant in six-packs or any pots. You will have to order seed from specialty catalogs and grow the plants yourself.

Planting

Seeding: Direct sow or sow in cold frame in fall

Transplanting: Spring

Spacing: 18–24"

Growing

Blue Eyes prefers **partial to light shade** in **moist, humus-rich, well-drained** soil. It can tolerate full sun in cool-summer coastal areas.

Divide in spring, or in fall when the center of the plant begins to die out. Stem cuttings taken in spring will also be effective for propagating Blue Eyes.

Tips

Grow Blue Eyes in a woodland garden, border, or naturalized area. It makes an appealing groundcover under trees with high canopies.

The seeds require cold treatment before germination. This plant self-seeds once established.

Recommended

B. macrophylla is a mound-forming plant with large, heart-shaped leaves. It produces clusters of blue flowers with bright yellow centers. **'Dawson's White'** ('Variegata') has wide, cream-colored leaf margins and should only be grown in a shaded area with adequate moisture. The variegated form does not self-sow.

This plant is named after Swiss botanist Samuel Brunner (1790–1844).

B. macrophylla (above), 'Dawson's White' (below)

Blue Marguerite
Felicia, Blue Daisy
Felicia

Height: 10–24" **Spread:** 10"–4' **Flower color:** blue; yellow centers
Blooms: summer **Hardiness:** semi-hardy

BLUE MARGUERITE CAN BE THE BACKBONE OF ANY GARDEN. NOT
only is it free from most diseases and insect damage, it blooms from early
February through the end of November. My favorite use of this wonderful,
sun-loving perennial is growing it in untreated, unpainted clay pots. I have
several pots planted and when I need an extra bit of color in my yard, I transplant the flowers from the pot to the spot that needs it.

Planting

Seeding: Indoors in winter; direct sow in spring

Transplanting: Any time in coastal areas; April through June in the Central
Valley; from one-gallon containers

Spacing: 12–24"

Growing

Blue Marguerite likes **full sun**. The soil should be of **average fertility** and **well drained**. Ensure you provide adequate but not excessive water.

The key to keeping this plant looking its best is trimming. When plants are young, pinch the tips to promote bushiness. Regular deadheading will extend flowering. Cut the plants back in mid-July and then again in November to promote the production of new flowering wood. Be sure that you shear just under the spent blooms. If you prune too hard and get into more mature wood, the bloom cycle will be delayed. Take cuttings from the new fall growth to start new plants for the following spring. This method will save you the uncertainty of starting with seeds.

Because the plant blooms over a long time, it requires monthly feeding to keep the foliage its proper color.

Tips

With its sprawling habit, Blue Marguerite is well suited to rock gardens, bed edges, mixed containers and hanging moss baskets. It combines well with other low-spreading plants such as Basket-of-gold and the sweet potato vine cultivar 'Blackie.'

Recommended

F. amelloides forms a rounded, bushy mound and bears yellow-centered flowers in varied shades of blue. This woody-based perennial grows 12–24" tall and spreads 24"–4' or more. **'Astrid Thomas'** is a dwarf

variety with blue flowers. It grows 10" tall, with an equal spread. The cultivar **'Midnight'** has blue flowers and is the same size as the species.

Problems & Pests

Blue Marguerite is generally trouble free, although aphids cause occasional problems.

Blue Star Flower
Willow Blue Star
Amsonia

Height: 12–36" **Spread:** 12–36" **Flower color:** blue **Blooms:** late spring to mid-summer **Hardiness:** hardy

THE FLOWER CLUSTERS OF A BLUE STAR FLOWER ADD AN AIRY touch to the perennial bed and contrast well with other perennials. When planted with the bright colors of Blanket Flower, the contrast is striking. This plant is a good groundcover underneath Joe Pye Weed and other large perennials.

Planting

Seeding: Sow seeds in flats in cold frame in fall

Transplanting: Spring or fall

Spacing: 12" for *A. ciliata*, 24" for *A. orientalis*

Growing

Blue star flowers prefer **partial shade** where they are somewhat drought tolerant but tolerate full sun if well watered. In the Central Valley, blue star flowers will need to be in morning sun only. They prefer a **moist, well-drained** soil of **average to rich fertility**.

After flowering, cut back by one-third to avoid floppy plants and prevent zealous self-seeding. Propagate with softwood cuttings. Divide in early fall or spring.

Tips

The willow-like foliage of blue star flowers turns an attractive yellow-gold in fall. These plants love moist soil and make a beautiful addition at the side of a stream or pond.

Be sure to wash your hands thoroughly after handling blue star flower plants. Some people find the sap irritates the skin.

Recommended

A. ciliata grows 12–36" tall, spreads 12" and flowers in late spring to summer. The narrow, downy leaves cluster with the flowers at the end of the stems. This species is native to the southern United States.

A. orientalis (*Rhazya orientalis*) has gray-green leaves. This species bears violet-blue flowers in early to mid-summer. It grows 20–30" tall and 36" wide and has denser growth than *A. ciliata*. It is very easy to start from seed.

Problems & Pests

Blue star flowers may have occasional problems with rust.

These easy-to-grow and hardy perennials make excellent woodland plants, growing naturally at the margins between field and forest.

Butterfly Weed
Milkweed
Asclepias

Height: 18–42" **Spread:** 12–24" **Flower color:** orange, yellow, red
Blooms: mid-summer to fall **Hardiness:** hardy

I ONCE MADE A BOUQUET OUT OF A BUNCH OF BUTTERFLY WEED blooms and put it on the outside deck while I straightened up an area in the house. When I returned to the bouquet, it was loaded with butterflies. I was tempted to bring the arrangement into the house, butterflies and all, but thought better of it and waited until evening when the butterflies flew away before bringing the bouquet in. Butterfly weeds are native to the United States and add a very colorful accent to any perennial garden. The flowers make long-lasting cut flowers that liven up even the darkest of homes.

Planting

Seeding: Direct sow or start in cold frame in mid-March

Transplanting: Mid-March to mid-April

Spacing: 12–24"

Growing

Butterfly weeds prefer **full sun** in any **well-drained, moderate to infertile** soil. Planting in infertile soil will help keep the plants from overgrowing their place. These plants are drought tolerant once established but don't mind occasional deep watering.

The deep taproot makes division difficult. Remove the plantlets that grow around the base of the plants for propagation.

These plants are slow to start in spring. Place a marker beside the plant in fall so you won't forget the plant is there and inadvertently dig it up in spring.

Tips

Use butterfly weeds in meadow plantings, borders, on dry banks, in neglected areas and in wildflower, cottage and butterfly gardens. These plants yield excellent cut flowers.

The milky sap is **poisonous** and may irritate exposed skin. Do not eat any parts of these plants.

Recommended

A. curassavica (Blood Flower) is an evergreen, woody-based plant growing to a height of 36–42" and spreading 24". Flattened clusters of red to red-orange flowers give way to erect, showy fruits that make an attractive fall feature.

A. tuberosa forms a clump of upright, leafy stems. It grows 18–36" tall and spreads 12–24". It bears clusters of orange flowers. The cultivar **'Gay Butterflies'** bears orange, yellow or red flowers.

A. curassavica (above),
A. tuberosa with *Liatris* (below)

Asclepias *species will attract butterflies to your garden. These plants are a major food source for the Monarch butterfly.*

California Poppy

Eschscholzia

Height: 8–18" **Spread:** 6–12" **Flower color:** orange, yellow, red, pink, cream
Blooms: spring to summer **Hardiness:** hardy

AS A THIRD-GENERATION CALIFORNIAN, I AM NOT QUITE READY to accept what hybridizers are doing to the color of California Poppy. From my childhood I have fond memories of fields of golden orange flowers that covered much of California's landscape and roadsides. At one time they were deer resistant, but as deer get crowded into smaller areas, they have started to eat the state's flower, so there are fewer and fewer wild stands of this flower. I encourage everyone to plant this wonderful flower anywhere they can in their gardens. California Poppy adapts to all but the worst garden conditions.

California Poppy is the state flower of California.

Planting

Seeding: Direct sow mid-spring or fall

Spacing: 6–12"

Growing

California Poppy prefers **full sun** but tolerates some shade. The soil should be of **poor or average fertility** and **well drained**. With too rich a soil, the plants will be lush and green but will bear few, if any, flowers. California Poppy requires a lot of water for germination and development of young plants. Until they are flowering, provide the plants with regular and frequent watering. Once they begin flowering they are drought tolerant, but providing adequate water will lengthen the bloom period. Do not overwater.

Never start this plant indoors because it dislikes having its roots disturbed. California Poppy will sprout quickly when planted directly in the garden. Sow seeds in early fall for blooms in spring or in early spring for blooms in summer.

Tips

California Poppy can be included in beds and borders, but regular dead-heading is required to keep it looking neat. This plant self-seeds wherever it is planted; it is perfect for naturalizing in a meadow garden or rock garden where it will come back year after year. The cultivars will not come true to seed.

Recommended

E. californica forms a mound of delicate, feathery, blue-green foliage and bears satiny orange or yellow flowers. This plant grows 8–18" tall and 6–12" wide. **'Ballerina'** has a mixture of colors and semi-double or double flowers. **'Chiffon'** forms compact plants, up to 8", that bear semi-double flowers in pink and apricot. **'Mission Bells'** bears ruffled double and semi-double flowers in mixed and solid shades of orange, yellow, red, cream and pink. **'Thai Silk'** bears flowers in pink, red, yellow and orange with silky, wavy-edged petals. The compact plants grow 8–10" tall.

These light-sensitive flowers close at night and on overcast days.

Candle Larkspur

Delphinium

Height: 3–8' **Spread:** 18–36"
Flower color: blue, purple, pink,
red, yellow, white, bicolors
Blooms: late spring, summer;
may bloom again in fall if cut
back **Hardiness:** hardy

CANDLE LARKSPURS ARE
some of the easiest spike-
type flowers to grow. Once
established, these plants
add a beautiful display to
the garden, and they are
wonderful, long-lasting cut
flowers. Perfect drainage is
the key to successful plantings.
Watch for sowbugs and pill bugs
(rolly pollys) around your candle
larkspur plants. These are beneficial insects that feed on decaying
organic matter. While they
won't damage the candle larkspur, their presence indicates
some sort of damage or
insect attacks.

Delphinium *comes from*
Delphis, *the Greek word for*
dolphin. The petals of the
flowers somewhat resemble
the nose and fins of that
creature.

Planting

Seeding: Direct sow once soil reaches 55° F; indoors in cold frame earlier

Transplanting: Spring to early summer or early fall; from jumbo six-packs

Spacing: 18–24"

Growing

Grow in a **full sun** location well protected from strong winds. The soil should be **fertile, moist, humus rich** and **neutral to slightly alkaline** with **excellent drainage**. These heavy feeders require fertilizer twice a year, in spring and summer. They love well-rotted manure or chicken manure mixed into the soil. Adding superphosphate or 0-10-10 to the soil mix will help strengthen the plants and possibly avoid staking.

D. x *belladonna* hybrid (above)
D. x *elatum* hybrid (below)

The tall flower spikes have hollow centers and are easily broken if exposed to the wind. Each flower spike needs to be individually staked. Stakes should be installed as soon as a flower spike reaches 12" in height. You can use wire tomato cages or thick bamboo stakes for this purpose.

When transplanting candle larkspurs, plant with crown at soil level to avoid crown rot.

Candle larkspurs require division each spring to extend their life and keep them vigorous. The plants may not come true to type from collected seed, so you might prefer to use purchased seed. If you are harvesting your own seed, refrigerate seeds for a month before planting.

D. x *elatum* hybrid (below)

Tips

Candle larkspurs are classic cottage-garden plants. Their height and need for staking relegate them to the back of the border, where they make a magnificent blue-toned backdrop for warmer-colored flowers such as poppies and black-eyed Susans.

To encourage a second flush of smaller blooms in fall, remove the first flower spikes once they begin to fade and before they set seed. Cut them off just above the foliage. New shoots will begin to grow and the old foliage will fade back. The old growth may then be cut right back to allow new growth to fill in.

Recommended

D. x *belladonna* (Belladonna Hybrids) grows 36–48" tall and spreads 18–24". It bears bright blue flowers in early to late summer. It is a low, well-branched, airy cultivar with an open habit and does not require staking.

D. x *elatum* (Elatum Hybrids) grows 4–6' tall and 24–36" wide. In early to mid-summer, tall, densely flowered spikes bloom in blue, red, pink, white, yellow, violet and purple. **Pacific Giants** are fast-growing hybrids with *D.* x *elatum* as one of the parents. They reach a height of 5–8' and spread 30–36". Pacific Giants are short-lived and are often grown as annuals or biennials. They flower from seed the first year in shades of white, blue, purple and pink. Many named selections are available.

Problems & Pests

Slugs and snails are the worst problems for candle larkspur plants and may eradicate these plants from your garden; take protective measures in early spring. Occasional problems with cyclamen mites, powdery mildew, bacterial and fungal leaf spots, gray mold, crown and root rot, white rot, rust, white smut, leaf smut and damping off are also possible. Healthy plants are less susceptible to problems.

These plants are so gorgeous in bloom that you can build a garden or plan a party around their flowering.

D. x *belladonna* hybrid (above)
D. x *elatum* hybrid (below)

Candytuft
Iberis

Height: 4–12" **Spread:** 10–24" **Flower color:** white
Blooms: Mid-January through mid-March **Hardiness:** hardy

CANDYTUFT FORMS A MOUND OF TINY DARK GREEN LEAVES, AND when it bursts into bloom, the plant is covered with blossoms. It is best used as a border around perennial beds or as a permanent planting around an annual bed. It requires only an occasional shearing after the bloom cycle to keep it looking sharp. It makes a wonderful evergreen addition to moss baskets. Adding red cyclamen to the mix makes a wonderful color combination that will take you through the winter.

Planting
Seeding: Sow in containers or direct sow in fall

Transplanting: Fall

Spacing: 6–12"

Growing

Candytuft prefers **full sun** but toler-ates partial shade. The soil should be of **poor to average fertility, moist, well drained** and **neutral to alkaline.** Candytuft should be sheared back by about one-third once it has fin-ished flowering to promote new, compact growth. Every two or three years it should be sheared back by one-half to two-thirds to discourage the development of too much woody growth and to encourage abundant flowering.

As the stems spread outwards, they may root where they touch the ground. These rooted ends may be cut away from the central plant, and in this way you can avoid having to divide the entire plant. In spring, cut away any brown sections result-ing from winter damage. Division is rarely required.

Tips

Use Candytuft as an edging plant, in borders and rock gardens, along path edges, in the crevices of rock walls and with spring-blooming bulbs.

Recommended

I. sempervirens is a spreading, ever-green plant with clusters of tiny, white flowers. It grows 6–12" tall and spreads 12–24". **'Autumn Snow'** bears white flowers in spring and fall. **'Little Gem'** is a compact, spring-flowering plant that reaches only 4–6" in height and 10" in width. **'Snowflake'** is a mounding plant with larger foliage than the species. It bears large white flowers on short stems in spring and usually again in fall.

Problems & Pests

Occasional problems with slugs, snails, caterpillars, damping off, gray mold and fungal leaf spot are possible.

Cape Fuchsia

Phygelius

Height: 24"–4' **Spread:** 3–5'
Flower color: orange, red, yellow,
peach; some cultivars have yellow
throats **Blooms:** summer to fall
Hardiness: semi-hardy

CAPE FUCHSIAS ARE WONDER-
FUL for filling in bare spots in perennial gardens. Like the related flowers
beard tongues and snapdragons, cape
fuchsia blooms are long-lasting, although
somewhat messy, as cut flowers. These
plants tend to spread, but not to the
point of invasiveness. Their spreading is
easy to control by digging up the shallow roots, which you can then share with
friends and neighbors.

Planting

Seeding: Sow in containers in cold frame
in spring; seedlings may vary in color from
parent plants.

Transplanting: Spring through summer;
from 4" pots or one-gallon containers

Spacing: 3–5'

*After your cape fuchsia
blooms, cut the old flower
stalks to the ground to keep
it looking clean and to
encourage new blooms.*

Growing

Cape fuchsias prefer **full sun** or **light shade** and **well-drained, moist, fertile** soil. Protect from winter freezing with a dry mulch. In hot areas, apply a summertime mulch.

Cape fuchsias spread naturally by rhizomes and by prostrate stems that send down roots where they touch the ground. Divide in spring. Dig up and re-plant rooted suckers to propagate. Named varieties should be propagated by cuttings or ground layering. Take softwood cuttings in late spring or early summer.

Tips

Use cape fuchsias at the back of perennial or mixed borders, or try them in a shrub border where their woody habits will fit well.

Recommended

P. capensis is an upright, open, woody perennial that reaches a height of 3–4' and a spread of 4–5'. It produces open clusters of orange to red flowers. It is a parent of *P.* x *rectus*.

P. x *rectus* grows 4' tall and 5' wide. **'African Queen'** bears pale red to orange flowers with a yellow throat. **'Moonraker'** has pale yellow flowers. **'Pink Elf'** is a smaller cultivar growing 24–30" tall and spreading 36". It has pale pink to dark pink flowers. **'Salmon Leap'** bears deeply lobed orange flowers.

Problems & Pests

Weevils and capsid bugs may cause occasional problems.

'Moonraker' (this page)

Cardinal Flower
Lobelia

Height: 2–5' **Spread:** 9–24" **Flower color:**
maroon, red, pink, white, blue, blue-purple
Blooms: summer to fall
Hardiness: hardy to semi-hardy

THESE FLOWERS AND THEIR VIVID COLOR
just have to be the joy of a garden when summer
arrives. When annuals and some perennials are
showing the stress of spring, these beautiful
plants add color like the Fourth of July. The reds
combine well with almost any other perennial.
A wonderfully patriotic combination is *Lobelia
cardinalis*, white Shasta Daisy and a blue beard
tongue. You'll have to hold your hand over your
heart every time you go by the garden.

Planting
Seeding: Once seeds are ripe, direct sow or sow
in containers in cold frame

Transplanting: Spring

Spacing: 12"

Growing

Cardinal flowers do well in **full sun** or **partial shade**. *L. siphilitica* can take full sun along the coast but in the Sacramento Valley requires protection from excessive heat. Afternoon shade is imperative in this location. The soil should be **fertile, slightly acidic** and **moist**. Cardinal flowers also grow well in boggy soils. Divide in summer by lifting the entire plant and removing the new rosettes growing at the base. Re-plant them immediately in the garden. Spreading a light mulch and leaving the stems on the plant will help ensure winter survival. Remove the mulch in spring.

Pinch the plants in early summer for more compact growth. Deadheading may encourage a second set of blooms. If you deadhead, allow a few flower spikes to remain to spread their seeds. Don't worry too much, though—the lower flowers on a spike are likely to set seed before the top flowers are finished opening.

Tips

Cardinal flowers are ideal alongside a stream or pond. They may also be grown in a bog garden, as long as it doesn't dry out for extended periods. Keep these plants at the back of the border so they can get support from lower-growing plants.

Cardinal flowers may require more acidic soil than other plants growing near a pond. In this case, plant in a container of acidic soil and sink it into the ground at the edge of the pond.

L. cardinalis (this page)

Recommended

L. cardinalis (Cardinal Flower) forms an erect clump of bronze-green leaves. It grows 24"–4' tall, spreads 12–24" and bears spikes of bright red flowers. 'Alba' has white flowers. '**Ruby Slippers**' has deep ruby red flowers. '**Twilight Zone**' has light pink flowers.

L. siphilitica (Blue Cardinal Flower) forms an erect clump with bright green foliage. It grows 24"–4' tall and spreads 12–18". It bears spikes of blue to bright blue flowers from mid-summer to fall. 'Alba' (forma *albiflora*) has white flowers.

L. x *speciosa* includes hybrids with undetermined parentage. Some of these hybrids, which may grow 4–5' tall and 12" wide, display red foliage and flowers. '**Compliment**' series

L. cardinalis (above), *L. siphilitica* (below)

grows to 30" and spreads 9", bearing flowers in scarlet, deep red or blue-purple. **'Dark Crusader'** grows 24–36" tall and 12" wide. It has maroon to dark purple stems and leaves and deep red blooms. **'Queen Victoria'** forms a clump of reddish stems with maroon foliage and scarlet flowers. It grows about 36" tall and spreads 12". Ensure adequate water for these selections.

Problems & Pests

Occasional problems with slugs, rust and leaf spot are possible. To reduce potential problems, water in the morning, allowing the plant to go through the night dry.

Lobelia *was named after Flemish botanist Mathias de l'Obel (1538–1616).*

Catmint

Nepeta

Height: 12–36" **Spread:** 18–36" **Flower color:** blue, purple, white, pink
Blooms: late spring to summer **Hardiness:** hardy

THESE HARDY PERENNIALS ARE SOME OF THE MOST FORGIVING.
All catmints require only minimal watering during the warm summer
months. The plants also benefit from an occasional feeding with organic
fertilizer during the growing season. When *N.* x *faassenii* is used as a groundcover combined with other low-growing
fragrant herbs, the flowering season of
the mix extends from May
through October.

Planting

Seeding: Most popular hybrids and cultivars are sterile and cannot be grown from seed

Transplanting: April through July; from 4" pots

Spacing: 18–24"

Growing

Catmints grow well in **full sun** or **partial shade**. The soil should be of **average fertility** and **well drained**. Plants will tend to flop over in rich soil. Once the plants are almost finished blooming, you may cut them back by one-third to one-half to encourage new growth and possibly a second bloom in late summer or fall. In late winter cut the plant back hard to make space for the new growth. Divide in spring or fall when the growth begins to look too dense. Propagate by division or by stem cuttings taken in spring before any flower buds form.

N. x faassenii (this page)

Catmint has long been cultivated for its reputed medicinal and culinary qualities.

Tips

Catmints can be used to edge borders and pathways and can be combined successfully with roses in cottage gardens and herb gardens.

If you grow *N. cataria* (Catnip) be aware that many cats are extremely attracted to this plant. If you don't want cats in your garden, you might want to think twice before including *N. cataria* in your plans. Cats do like the other species, but not to the same extent. If you find you are attracting too many cats to your garden, here is a non-toxic method for feline control. Put short, sharp bamboo stakes in the ground, leaving about two inches exposed to discourage cat damage. Just remember you put the sticks there if you're taking cuttings.

Recommended

N. x *faassenii* forms a clump of upright and spreading stems 12" tall and 12–18" wide. It bears spikes of blue or purple flowers in late spring to early summer. This hybrid and its cultivars are sterile and cannot be grown from seed. **'Dawn to Dusk'** has pink flowers. **'Dropmore'** grows to 18" tall and 24–36" wide with gray-green foliage and light purple flowers. **'Snowflake'** grows 12" tall and 18" wide and bears pure white flowers.

N. **'Six Hills Giant'** is a large, vigorous plant. It grows 36" tall, or taller, and spreads 24". It bears large spikes of lavender blue flowers in summer.

Problems & Pests

These plants are pest free, except for an occasional cat or bout of leaf spot.

It is no mystery why 'cat' is part of the common name—many cats love these plants! Cloth toys stuffed with the dried leaves can amuse kittens and cats for hours.

'Six Hills Giant' (above)

Columbine

Aquilegia

Height: 24–36" **Spread:** 12–18" **Flower color:** red, yellow, pink, purple, blue, white, orange; color of spurs often differs from that of petals
Blooms: spring, summer **Hardiness:** hardy

NATIVE COLUMBINES CAN BE FOUND IN MANY OF THE mountainous regions of Northern California. The native variety in the state has a bright yellow center with bright red spurs. Columbine plants look great in any woodland garden. They combine wonderfully with plaintain lilies, ferns and other shade-loving plants. They tolerate full sun along the coast but need protection from the heat in the Central Valley. 'McKana Giants' are the most widely available, in six-packs in early spring and in 4" pots in late spring and early summer.

Planting

Seeding: Direct sow in spring

Transplanting: Spring to early summer

Spacing: About 18"

Growing

Columbines grow well in **full sun** or **partial shade.** For the best performance, the soil should be **fertile, moist** and **well drained,** but columbines adapt well to most soil conditions. These plants self-seed, and young seedlings can be transplanted. Division is not required but can be done to propagate desirable forms. They may take a while to recover as they dislike having their roots disturbed.

Tips

Use columbines in a rock garden, a formal or casual border or a naturalized or woodland garden.

Columbines self-seed but are in no way invasive. Each year a few new plants may turn up near the parent plant. If you have a number of different columbines planted near each other, you may wind up with a new hybrid because these plants cross-breed easily. The variety of flower colors is the most interesting result. The new seedlings may not be identical to the parents and may even revert to the original species.

The dainty, suspended flowers of columbines attract butterflies and hummingbirds.

'McKana Giants' (above)

'Double Pleat' (above)

Recommended

A. caerulea (Rocky Mountain Columbine) grows 24–36" tall and spreads 12". In late spring to mid-summer it bears large, bicolored blue and white nodding flowers with narrow spurs—very showy for a wild species. For good results grow this plant in light shade.

A. formosa (Western Columbine, Red Columbine) grows 24–36" tall and 18" wide. The flowers are borne in late spring to early summer and are bicolored red and yellow (sometimes orange) with large, upright red spurs. Western Columbine is the state flower of Colorado and is native to California and other western states.

A. x *hybrida* (*A.* x *cultorum*) (Hybrid Columbine) forms mounds of delicate foliage. Many groups of hybrids

have been developed for their showy flowers of varied colors. When the exact parentage of a plant is uncertain it is grouped under this heading. **'Double Pleat'** (Double Pleat Hybrids) grows 30–32" tall and 12–18" wide. It bears double flowers in combinations of blue and white or pink and white. **'Dragonfly'** (Dragonfly Hybrids) has a wide range of flower colors on compact plants up to 24" tall and 12" in spread. **'McKana Giants'** (McKana Hybrids) are popular and bear flowers in yellow, pink, red, purple, mauve and white. The plants grow up to 36" tall.

'McKana Giants' (this page)

Problems & Pests

Mildew is a problem during wet weather, and rust can be troublesome during dry weather. Other potential problems are fungal leaf spot, aphids, caterpillars and leaf miners.

Columbines are short-lived perennials that seed freely and establish themselves in unexpected, and often charming, locations. If you wish to keep a particular form, you must preserve it carefully through frequent division or root cuttings.

Copper Canyon Daisy
Mexican Marigold
Tagetes

Height: 3–6' **Spread:** 3–6' **Flower color:** golden yellow to orange
Blooms: spring to fall **Hardiness:** semi-hardy

MANY PEOPLE CONSIDER THE ANNUAL MARIGOLD AN INSECT repellant. This may be true in some locations, but not in Northern California. In most cases I find that annual marigolds can harbor whiteflies and other undesirable insects. Copper Canyon Daisy is the marigold most likely to repel insects (and some people). You either love the fragrance or hate it. I find the pungent lemony fragrance from the foliage of this plant positively delightful. Copper Canyon Daisy is one of the few plants that I consider a must for spring through fall color. And yes, in some frost-free areas it will bloom year-round.

Marigolds are said to release substances into the soil that help repel garden insect pests.

Planting

Seeding: Indoors in mid- to late winter; direct sow after last frost

Transplanting: Mid-March through mid-July

Spacing: 3–4'

Growing

Grow Copper Canyon Daisy in **full sun** in **well-drained, fertile** soil. A frost-free, sheltered location is best. This plant can be cut back to maintain a desired shape. Remove all dead or damaged stems and leaves in March. Copper Canyon Daisy will die back to the ground if temperatures drop below 22° F. It will re-sprout from the roots if the soil doesn't freeze.

Copper Canyon Daisy is easy to propagate from cuttings.

Tips

Copper Canyon Daisy can be used in beds and borders. Try it along a path where the fragrant foliage can be brushed in passing.

Recommended

T. lemmonii (*T. palmeri*) is a short-lived, shrubby, upright to slightly sprawling perennial with finely dissected leaves. When brushed against or bruised, the leaves emit a strong fragrance.

Problems & Pests

This plant may have problems with gray mold, slugs and snails.

Coral Bells
Alum Root
Heuchera

Height: 12"–4' **Spread:** 12–18" **Flower color:** red, pink, white, purple
Blooms: spring, summer **Hardiness:** hardy

MY GRANDMOTHER GREW CORAL BELLS IN THE 1930s, AND THEY
seemed to be in bloom all the time. Since then they've been transplanted to
new homes with various members of my family and have proven that they
can grow anywhere in Northern California, from Ukiah to Sacramento to
Lincoln. When my parents' coral bells were destroyed by rabbits and wild
pigs, my sister gave them a tub full of roots to plant in their new home in
Loomis. Coral bells plants have survived in new locations even when their
owners passed away; they became very special to me after my sister died.
Coral bells are certainly long-lived perennials.

Planting

Seeding: Start species, but not cultivars, in spring or fall in a cold frame

Transplanting: Spring

Spacing: 12–18"

Growing

Coral bells prefer **light or partial
shade.** Foliage colors can bleach out
in full sun, and plants can become
leggy in full shade. The soil should
be of **average to rich fertility,
humus rich, neutral to alkaline,
moist** and **well drained.** Good air
circulation is essential. If the soil is
acidic, horticultural lime should be
applied each year.

'Palace Purple' (above & center)

Remove spent flowers to prolong
the blooming period. Every two or
three years coral bells should be dug
up to remove the oldest, woodiest
roots and stems. The plants may be
divided at this time, if desired, then
re-planted with the crown just
above soil level. Cultivars may be

'Firefly' (below)

'Palace Purple' (above), 'Firefly' (below)

propagated by division in spring or fall, or by stem cuttings in spring.

Tips

Use coral bells as edging plants, clustered in woodland gardens or as groundcovers in low-traffic areas. Combine different foliage types for an interesting display.

Coral bells have a strange habit of pushing themselves up out of the soil—mulch in fall if the plants begin heaving from the ground.

Recommended

Most of the cultivars listed here are hybrids developed from crossing the various species. They have been grouped for convenience with one of their acknowledged parents.

H. x *brizioides* is a group of mound-forming hybrids developed through extensive crossbreeding for their attractive flowers. They grow 12–30" tall and spread 12–18". **'Chatterbox'** has bright reddish pink flowers. **'Firefly'** grows up to 24" with densely mounded, light green foliage and red blooms on wire-like stems. **'June Bride'** has large, white flowers. **'Raspberry Regal'** is a larger plant, growing up to 48" tall. The foliage is strongly marbled and the flowers are bright red.

H. micrantha (Crevice Heuchera) is a mounding, clump-forming plant up to 36" tall. The foliage is gray-green and the flowers are white. The species is not often found in gardens, but there are many common cultivars. **'Bressingham Hybrids'** are compact plants that can be started from seed. Flowers will be pink or red. 'Chocolate Ruffles' has ruffled, glossy, brown foliage with purple undersides that give the leaves a bronzed appearance. The cultivar var. *diversifolia* 'Palace Purple' is popular. It is compact, 18–20" tall, and has deep purple foliage and white blooms. It can be started from seed, but only some of the seedlings will be true to type. 'Pewter Moon' has light pink flowers and silvery leaves with bronze-purple veins.

H. sanguinea is the hardiest *Heuchera* species. It forms a low-growing mat of foliage 12–18" tall, with an equal spread. The dark green foliage is marbled with silver. The red, pink or white flowers are borne in summer. 'Cherry Splash' is appropriately named. It reaches 16" in height and bears cherry red flowers. The foliage is splashed with splotches of gold and white. 'Coral Cloud' has pinkish red flowers and glossy, crinkled leaves. 'Frosty' has red flowers and silver variegated foliage. 'Northern Fire' has red flowers and leaves mottled with silver.

Problems & Pests

Healthy coral bells have very few problems, although mealybugs may cause serious damage. Stressed plants may also be afflicted with foliar nematodes, powdery mildew, rust or leaf spot.

These woodland plants will enhance your garden with their bright colors, attractive foliage and airy sprays of flowers.

'Palace Purple' (below)

Coreopsis
Tickseed
Coreopsis

Height: 6–36" **Spread:** 12–24" **Flower color:** yellow **Blooms:** late spring to fall **Hardiness:** hardy, semi-hardy

THESE PLANTS ARE THE STARS OF THE GARDENING SHOW IN THE Sacramento Valley during hot summers. The profuse habit of these plants to form seeds will attract many different kinds of seed-eating birds. Keep your eyes open, because you may find birds eating in your yard that you have never seen before. The birds will not bother the plants and in fact will help control the insect population. The flowers hold up quite well in arrangements.

Planting

Seeding: Direct sow in spring, indoors in winter; soil at 55–61° F. Sow seed of *C. maritima* in fall or mid-summer in flats for transplanting in late October.

Transplanting: Spring or late fall

Spacing: 12–18"

Growing

Grow coreopsis plants in **full sun**. The soil should be **average, sandy** and **well drained**. Coreopsis will die in moist, cool locations. Good drainage is the key to success with this plant in cooler areas. Soil that is overly fertile causes floppy growth.

Shear plants by one-half in late spring for more compact growth. Daily deadheading will keep plants in constant summer bloom. Use scissors to snip out tall stems. Frequent division may be required to keep plants vigorous.

C. verticillata

Deadheading your coreopsis plant will encourage more blooms, brightening your garden through summer and fall.

'Moonbeam'

'Moonbeam' (left)

Tips

Coreopsis plants are versatile, useful in formal and informal borders and in a meadow planting or cottage garden. These plants look nice individually or in large groups.

If plants blacken from frost, remove the blackened foliage in fall to prevent slugs from using it as a nursery.

Recommended

C. auriculata (Mouse-eared Tickseed) is low growing and well suited to rock gardens or fronts of borders. It grows 12–24" tall and creeps outwards without becoming invasive. **'Nana'** grows to 6–8" tall and bears yellow flowers from late spring to early fall.

C. lanceolata grows 24" tall and spreads 18". Yellow-centered yellow flowers bloom from late spring to mid-summer. This species produces a large number of flowers and can create a blanket of gold if planted in masses. **'Brown Eyes'** grows to 24" tall and bears yellow flowers marked with a reddish purple ring. **'Goldfink'** grows 8–12" tall and bears golden yellow flowers.

C. maritima (Sea Dahlia) has stout, branched, fleshy stems 12–36" tall and 12–24" wide. Deep yellow flowers are borne for an extended period from early spring to summer; they make nice long-stemmed cut flowers. This wind-resistant plant is an excellent choice for a coastal garden but may not do well inland.

C. verticillata (Thread-leaf Coreopsis) is an attractive, mound-forming plant with finely divided foliage. It grows 24–32" tall and 18" wide. This species is long-lived and will need dividing less frequently than most other species. Divide if some of the plant seems to be dying. This species naturalizes easily but can also become invasive. Pulling or hoeing can easily control offspring plants. '**Moonbeam**' forms a compact mound of delicate foliage. The flowers are creamy yellow.

Problems & Pests

Occasional problems with slugs, bacterial spot, gray mold, aster yellows, powdery mildew, downy mildew and fungal spot are possible.

Mass plant coreopsis to fill in a dry, exposed bank where nothing else will grow, and you will enjoy the bright, sunny flowers all summer long.

C. verticillata (above),
C. lanceolata cultivar with *Crocosmia* (below)

Cranesbill
Hardy Geranium
Geranium

Height: 6–30" **Spread:** 12–36" **Flower color:** white, red, pink, purple, blue
Blooms: spring to fall **Hardiness:** hardy

IF YOU EVER MEET A COLLECTOR OF THESE WONDERFUL PLANTS,
you will have a memorable experience. Collectors are rabid but forgivable. I
think it is because people often confuse plants of the genus *Geranium* with
those of the genus *Pelargonium* and can't understand why collectors of the
true geranium get upset with the statement, 'Geraniums are Geraniums.'
These extremely hardy plants can be planted in sun or shade and be expected
to do quite well. The plants are grown as much for their foliage as for their
flowers. When purchasing these plants, read the label or do a little research,
as the varieties have different growth habits.

Planting

Seeding: Start species from seed in early fall or spring; cultivars and hybrids may not come true to type

Transplanting: Spring or fall

Spacing: 6–24"

Growing

Cranesbills prefer to grow in **full sun** to **light shade**. A **moist** soil of **average fertility** and with **good drainage** is preferred, but most conditions are tolerated except waterlogged soil. These plants dislike hot weather and will benefit from afternoon shade. Shear back spent blooms for a second set of flowers. If the foliage is looking ratty, prune it back in late summer to rejuvenate.

Propagate by taking small, rooted pieces from the edge of the clump or by stem cuttings in summer. Cranesbills don't divide very easily because they have a large central root. If you must divide, do so in early spring when the clump becomes crowded.

Tips

These long-flowering plants are great in the border, filling in the spaces between shrubs and other larger plants and keeping the weeds down. They can be included in rock gardens and woodland gardens and mass planted as groundcovers.

Recommended

G. incanum is a mound-forming, evergreen perennial 6–15" tall and 24–36" wide. It has lace-like, fragrant foliage and produces magenta

G. incanum (above), *G. sanguineum* cultivar (below)

The Greek word for crane is geranos, *the source of both the genus and the common names. The beak-like fruits of these plants resemble a crane's bill.*

to deep pink flowers with darker veins in late spring to early fall. This species is good for a warm, sunny spot in the garden. It readily self-seeds and may become a pest. It is only marginally frost hardy.

G. x *magnificum* (Showy Geranium) is a vigorous, clump-forming perennial 24–30" tall and wide. In late spring to early summer, it produces violet-blue flowers heavily veined in dark red to dark purple. This sterile hybrid must be propagated by division or cuttings.

G. phaeum (Dusky Cranesbill, Mourning Widow) forms clumps 24–30" tall and 18" wide. The foliage often has brown or purple-brown markings. Clusters of white-centered dusky purple, deep maroon to almost black flowers bloom from spring to fall. This plant prefers a moist, shady location. **Forma** *album* bears white flowers. '**Lily Lovell**' has large, white-centered deep purple-maroon flowers. **Var.** *lividum* bears light pink to light mauve flowers and has unmarked foliage. '**Samobor**'

'Plenum Violaceum' (above),
G. sanguineum cultivar (below)

has strongly maroon-marked foliage and bears light maroon blooms. '**Variegatum**' has foliage with irregular yellow margins and pink blotches.

G. pratense (Meadow Cranesbill) forms an upright clump 18–30" tall and 24–36" wide. It bears white, blue or light purple flowers from late spring to summer. It self-seeds freely. '**Mrs. Kendall Clarke**' bears rose pink flowers with blue-gray veining. '**Plenum Violaceum**' bears purple double flowers for a longer period than the species because it sets no seed.

G. sanguineum (Bloody Cranesbill, Bloodred Cranesbill) forms a dense, mounding clump of dark green foliage that turns blood red in fall. It grows 6–18" tall and spreads 18–30". Bright magenta flowers are borne in late spring to mid-summer and sporadically until fall. '**Album**' has white flowers and a more open habit than other cultivars. '**Alpenglow**' has bright rosy red flowers and dense foliage. '**Elsbeth**' has light pink flowers with dark pink veins. '**Shepherd's Warning**' is a dwarf plant growing to 6" tall and up to 12" wide with rosy pink flowers. **Var.** *striatum* is heat and drought tolerant. It has pale pink blooms with blood red veins.

Problems & Pests

Bacterial blight, downy and powdery mildew, gray mold, leaf spot, leaf miners and slugs may cause occasional problems.

G. sanguineum var. *striatum* (above)

Dame's Rocket
Sweet Rocket
Hesperis

Height: 36" **Spread:** 24–36" **Flower color:** purple, lilac, white
Blooms: late spring to summer **Hardiness:** hardy

DAME'S ROCKET IS ONE OF THE BEST PERENNIALS FOR FRAGRANCE and attracts some unusual butterflies such as the Mourning Cloak. Dame's Rocket combines well with Euryops Daisy and ornamental grasses and with the tropical accents of Bear's Breeches. It looks best with more substantial plants which will balance the delicate form of Dame's Rocket.

Planting

Seeding: Direct sow in spring; plants will not flower until the following year

Transplanting: Spring or fall

Spacing: 18"

Growing

Grow Dame's Rocket in **full sun** or **partial shade**. In the Central Valley this plant does best when kept out of the afternoon sun. The soil should be **average to fertile, humus rich, moist** and **well drained**. This short-lived perennial is unlikely to need dividing. It self-seeds easily and will provide a constant supply of new plants.

Some population control may be needed once Dame's Rocket gets going. Thin out seedlings and trim back some of the plants before they set seed if too many offspring plants are beginning to pop up. Double-flowered varieties will not set seed but may be propagated from cuttings taken from near the base of the plant in spring. Replace old, worn-out plants with some of the new seedlings.

Tips

This plant is an excellent choice for a woodland garden or meadow planting. It looks good in a mixed border with other late-spring bloomers. Planting it along with late-flowering plants assures a colorful display into fall.

Recommended

H. matronalis is an upright, branched, short-lived, evergreen perennial that produces clusters of purple to lilac flowers. The fragrance is more pronounced during humid weather or in evenings. Var. *albiflora* has white flowers. 'Alba Plena' has white double flowers. 'Purpurea Plena' has purple double flowers.

Problems & Pests

Occasional problems with viruses, mildew, slugs, snails, flea beetles and caterpillars are possible.

Daylily

Hemerocallis

Height: 12"–6' **Spread:** 12"–4' **Flower color:** every color except blue and pure white **Blooms:** spring, summer **Hardiness:** hardy

THERE ARE SO MANY VARIETIES OF DAYLILIES ON THE MARKET that it is best to see them in bloom before purchasing. I have seen daylilies in neglected gardens on old estates. They are never watered nor cared for in any way yet are doing quite well. I have had several plants of one of the older varieties that was in the same location for 30 years and looked great every spring. For the hobbyist, seedling varieties can often times be more spectacular than the parent plants. It takes up to three years before you will see a bloom, but often the effort is worth it.

Planting

Seeding: Sow in containers in cold frame in fall or spring; hybrids and cultivars will not come true to type from seed

Transplanting: Spring

Spacing: 12–36"

Growing

Daylilies grow in any light from **full sun** to **full shade.** The deeper the shade, the fewer flowers will be produced. The soil should be **fertile, moist** and **well drained,** but these plants adapt to most conditions. They are drought tolerant and hard to kill once established. Feeding daylilies with an organic fertilizer twice a year, in spring and summer, will ensure an abundance of blooms.

Divide every two to three years in fall or spring to keep plants vigorous and to propagate them. They can be left indefinitely without dividing. If you are using evergreen varieties, they will be better looking plants if they are lifted and divided. Old-fashioned plants that die to the ground every year are self-grooming and don't require dividing.

Tips

These versatile plants can be part of almost any garden. Daylilies may be included in a border or used for erosion control on a bank or along a ditch. Smaller types may be used in small gardens or in containers. In a natural garden, daylilies may be planted in large masses or drifts.

Both the common name, daylily, and the genus name Hemerocallis—*from the Greek* hemera *('day') and* kallos *('beauty')—indicate that these lovely blooms last only one day.*

Deadhead to make small-flowered varieties bloom again. Be careful when deadheading purple-flowered varieties of daylilies, as they can stain fingers and clothes.

To have a bed of these beauties, observe the blooming habits of all the varieties. There are early-, mid- and late-season bloomers. Some of the early-blooming varieties can bloom again. Several varieties mixed in the same bed will produce flowers from spring through summer. Many local nurseries will be more than willing to help you plan a garden that will achieve this effect.

Recommended

The number of forms, colors and sizes of daylilies is almost infinite. The older varieties and species tend to have fragrant flowers while the newer ones do not, but the new daylilies have more color variety. Check with your local nursery or daylily grower to find out what's available. Tall types grow 24–48" tall and 24–36" wide, and the dwarf types grow 12–24" tall and wide. The following popular cultivars are available from seed catalogs and may be available in your local nursery.

'Hyperion' grows 48" tall and bears very fragrant yellow flowers in mid-summer.

'Starburst' series comes in a range of colors and grows to 36" tall.

'Stella d'Oro' grows 24" tall and bears yellow flowers for a long period. This evergreen cultivar does well in pots and as groundcover.

Alternate Species

H. fulva (Tawny Daylily) grows 3–6' tall and 4' wide. It bears rusty or tawny orange blooms. This species has become naturalized across most of the country.

H. lilioasphodelus (*H. flava*) (Lemon Daylily) grows 30–36" tall and spreads 18–36". The fragrant, lemon yellow flowers bloom in spring.

Problems & Pests

Daylilies are generally pest free but may be afflicted by rust, *Hemerocallis* gall midge, aphids, spider mites, thrips, slugs and snails.

H. fulva cultivar (above)

Dianthus
Pinks
Dianthus

Height: 6–18" **Spread:** 12–24" **Flower color:** pink, red, white
Blooms: spring, summer **Hardiness:** hardy

I REALLY ENJOY THE WONDERFUL FRAGRANCE OF THESE PLANTS.
Cottage Pinks and Allwood Pinks make great, fragrant additions to any bouquet or garden. The flowers of all pinks can be dried for aromatic additions to sachets. Allwood Pinks are wonderful, compact hybrids that do not die out in the center like the Cottage Pinks. When Cottage Pinks begin to die out in the center, take some tip cuttings and place them into the center of the clump. This keeps this plant from looking shabby as the summer goes on. Deadheading is a must to extend the bloom time for all *Dianthus* flowers.

Planting

Seeding: Sow seed in flats or direct sow in fall or early spring; cultivars do not come true to type from seed

Transplanting: Spring; best from six-packs not in bloom

Spacing: 10–20"

Growing

A location with **full sun** is preferable, but some light shade is tolerated. A **moist, light, well-drained, neutral or alkaline** soil is required. The most important factor in the successful cultivation of dianthus plants is drainage—these plants hate to stand in water. Mix a fair amount of planting mix or compost into the soil before planting. Make sure the rootball of each plant is scored so that the plants will have room to spread their roots. Frequent division, each year or two, will keep the plants vigorous.

Dianthus plants may be difficult to propagate by division. It is often easier to take cuttings in summer, once flowering has finished. Cuttings should be 1–3" long. Strip the lower leaves from the cutting. The cuttings should be kept humid but ventilated so that fungal problems do not set in.

Tips

Dianthus plants are excellent in rock gardens, on rock walls and as edging flowers for borders and walkways.

Deadheading as the flowers fade is a good way to prolong blooming, especially with Allwood Pinks.

D. plumarius cultivar (above), *D. plumarius* (below)

The ruffled petal edges appear to have been trimmed with pinking shears, giving rise to the alternative common name 'pinks.'

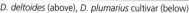

D. deltoides (above), *D. plumarius* cultivar (below)

Leave a few flowers in place to go to seed towards the end of the blooming period. The plants will self-seed quite easily. Seedlings may differ from the parent plants, often with new and interesting results.

Recommended

D.* x *allwoodii (Allwood Pinks) forms a compact mound and bears flowers in a wide range of colors. Cultivars generally grow 12–18" tall and 24" wide. **'Doris'** bears semi-double, salmon pink flowers with darker pink centers. It is popular as a cut flower. **'Laced Romeo'** bears spice-scented, red flowers with cream-margined petals. **'Sweet Wivelsfield'** bears fragrant, two-toned flowers in a variety of colors.

D. deltoides (Maiden Pink) grows 6–12" tall and about 12" wide. The plant forms a mat of foliage and flowers in spring. This is a popular species in rock gardens. It tolerates more shade than the other two species listed here but still requires 4–5 hours of sun per day. **'Brilliant'** ('Brilliancy', 'Brilliance') bears dark red flowers.

D. plumarius (Cottage Pink) is noteworthy for its role in the development of many popular cultivars known as Garden Pinks. The species has been found in European gardens for centuries. Cultivars are generally 12–18" tall and 24" wide, although smaller cultivars are available. They all flower in spring and into summer if deadheaded regularly. The flowers can be single, semi-double or fully double and are available in many colors. **'Dad's Favorite'** has red-edged, white double blooms.

Problems & Pests

Providing good drainage and air circulation will keep most fungal problems away. Occasional problems with slugs, blister beetles, sow bugs and grasshoppers are possible.

The tiny, delicate petals of dianthus blooms can be used to decorate cakes. Be sure to remove the white part at the base of the petal before using the petals or they will be bitter.

D. plumarius cultivar (above), *D. plumarius* (below)

Dusty Miller
Senecio

Height: 6"–4' **Spread:** 24"–4' **Flower color:** yellow, cream; grown for the silvery foliage **Blooms:** summer **Hardiness:** hardy to semi-hardy

ONE OF THE MOST BEAUTIFUL PLANTINGS I HAVE EVER SEEN WAS a mix of dusty millers with deep red *Pelargonium* plants. It was an outstanding display that went on for months. Dusty millers are among the easiest plants to grow in the garden. The lacy, gray, almost white, foliage adds a bounty of contrast to an almost all-green garden. If you allow the thistle-like blooms to open, they can be dried and used in arrangements, as can the leaves.

Planting

Seeding: Start seeds indoors in mid-winter or direct sow in spring; soil temperature 66° F

Transplanting: Spring

Spacing: 12–24"

Growing

Dusty millers prefer **full sun** but tolerate light shade. The soil should be of **average fertility** and **well drained**.

Pinch off the flowers before they bloom or they will detract from the foliage. If you leave the flowers, be aware that these plants are proficient self-seeders.

Shear the plants to keep them neat and compact, once a year in cooler areas and twice a year in milder areas. Ensure you cut low enough that any pruned stems will not be visible when the new foliage fills in.

Take stem cuttings from *S. cineraria* in mid- to late summer. The cuttings should be soft or just starting to ripen.

Tips

The soft, silvery, lacy leaves are the main feature of these plants, which are used primarily for edging. They are also used in beds, borders and containers. The silvery foliage makes a good backdrop for the brightly colored flowers of other plants.

Recommended

S. cineraria is an evergreen perennial 24–36" tall and 24" wide. It produces yellow flowers in summer. In the warmer areas it may flower all year. The following cultivars are smaller than the species, reaching 6–12" in height and spread. '**Cirrus**' has lobed, silvery green or white foliage. '**Silver Dust**' has deeply lobed, silvery white foliage. '**Silver Lace**' has delicate silvery white foliage that glows in the moonlight.

S. vira-vira is an evergreen, shrubby perennial growing 24"–4' tall and 3–4' wide. It has silver-white to bright white, finely dissected leaves. Keep this species in full sun for good foliage color and compact plants. Non-showy cream flowers are produced in summer.

Problems & Pests

Dusty millers are usually problem free, although they may occasionally suffer from rust. Remove afflicted plants and do not attempt to grow them again in the same location. These plants are deer proof.

S. vira-vira with *Aster novi-belgii* (above), 'Cirrus' (below)

Euphorbia
Cushion Spurge
Euphorbia

Height: 1–5' **Spread:** 18"–4' **Flower color:** yellow, green
Blooms: late winter to mid-spring **Hardiness:** hardy

ONE OF THE MOST SPECTACULAR WINTER-BLOOMING PERENNIALS, *E. characias* has recently become available from growers who see potential sales in January and February. On a cloudy day it adds a brilliant background to otherwise dull landscapes. *E. lathyris*, Gopher Plant, gets its name from its apparent ability to repel gophers and moles by means of its caustic sap, which is released when the animals damage its roots.

Planting

Seeding: Start fresh seed in a cold frame in spring

Transplanting: Spring or fall

Spacing: 18–36"

Growing

Euphorbias grow well in **full sun.** *E. lathyris* performs well in shade. The soil should be of **average fertility, moist, humus rich** and **well drained.** These plants are drought tolerant and can be invasive in too fertile a soil. Division is rarely required, and euphorbias dislike being disturbed once established.

Many species self-seed, but euphorbias can also be propagated by stem cuttings.

Tips

Use euphorbias in a mixed or herbaceous border, rock garden or woodland garden. It is a good idea to wear gloves when handling these

E. characias (above), *E. polychroma* (below)

The related E. pulcherrima *is the popular holiday Poinsettia. I have often been asked what to do with this plant after Christmas. My answer: toss it. Though it can be used as a houseplant, it is difficult to make it turn red again. The plants are native to warm, frost-free climates and will not survive where temperatures may drop below 30° F.*

plants because some people find that the sap irritates their skin. When using euphorbias as cut flowers, sear the cut ends with a flame or dip them in boiling water for a couple of seconds to stop the sticky white sap from running.

It is not the flowers that we admire on these attractive mounding plants, but rather the bracts (leaf-like structures), which turn a bright yellow.

Recommended

E. characias is an evergreen perennial with thick, woody-based stems. It grows 3–4' tall and wide and produces clusters of chartreuse flowers and purple nectar glands surrounded by green bracts at the ends of the stems. This is the earliest flowering of the species listed here. The stems are biennial, putting on leaves and height the first year and flowering the second year.

'Chameleon' (above), *E. characias* (below)

E. lathyris (Gopher Plant, Caper Spurge, Mole Plant) produces upright, sturdy, unbranched, biennial stems with blue-green leaves. The leaves appear in four rows spaced 90° apart like a stack of Xs. Each stem grows 3–5' tall and 12" wide and produces one cluster of yellow flowers surrounded by bright green bracts. The milky sap is caustic and poisonous. This species reseeds readily but is easily controlled by pulling out the unwanted plants.

Alternate Species

E. dulcis '**Chameleon**' is a mound-forming perennial growing 12–24" tall and wide. It bears yellow-green flowers and bracts, with the bracts and leaves later turning purple. The foliage is burgundy in spring, turning bronze-green over summer. This plant adds a wonderful contrast to the gray foliage of *Salvia clevelandii* and Mexican Sage.

E. polychroma (*E. epithimoides*) is a mounding, clump-forming perennial that grows 12–24" tall and 18–24" wide. The inconspicuous flowers are surrounded by long-lasting yellow bracts. The foliage turns shades of purple, red or orange in fall. There are several cultivars, though the species is more commonly available. Keep this plant out of the hottest afternoon sun. '**Candy**' has yellow bracts and flowers, but the leaves and stems are tinged with purple. '**Emerald Jade**' is a compact plant that grows to 14" in height. The bracts are yellow, but the flowers are bright green.

Problems & Pests

Aphids, spider mites and nematodes are possible problems, as is fungal root rot in poorly drained, wet soil.

E. polychroma (this page)

Evening Primrose

Oenothera

Height: 10–12" **Spread:** 24–36" or more **Flower color:** pink, white
Blooms: late spring to early fall **Hardiness:** hardy

EVENING PRIMROSE MAKES A COLORFUL ADDITION TO AREAS IN
the garden where other plants just don't grow. The plant goes dormant during the rainy season but pops right back in spring. The pink or white flowers
are a dominant feature of the plant, which has somewhat sparse foliage.
Evening Primrose may tend to spread where it isn't wanted, but weeding
once a year takes care of this problem. The flowers remain open during the
day, and established plantings give the impression of a massive pink cloud.
Evening Primrose combines well with Gaura, Mexican Sage and many members of the mint family.

Planting

Seeding: Sow seeds in containers in cold frame in early spring

Transplanting: Spring

Spacing: 24"

Growing

Grow Evening Primrose in **full sun.** Soil of **poor to average** fertility is preferred, but generally this plant is not too particular about soil conditions. Evening Primrose thrives in heavy clay soils to gravelly soils. In heavy clay soils the plant needs some peat moss or planting mix to start, but will do well without further help. Divide in spring as needed.

Evening Primrose spreads by rhizomes and may become invasive if the soil is too fertile. It is a very easy plant to cultivate.

Tips

Use Evening Primrose in the front or middle of a border. It may be used to edge a sunny path or to brighten a gravelly bank or rock garden.

Recommended

O. speciosa (Showy Evening Primrose) has fragrant white or pink flowers that open during the day. 'Alba' bears pure white flowers. 'Rosea' *(O. berlandieri, O. speciosa* var. *childsii)* (Mexican Evening Primrose) produces light pink to rose pink flowers.

Problems & Pests

Downy and powdery mildew, leaf gall, rust and leaf spot are possible problems. Roots may rot if the wet winter soil doesn't have adequate drainage, but plants usually recover.

False Rockcress
Rock Cress, Common Aubrieta
Aubrieta

Height: 2–6" **Spread:** 12–24" **Flower color:** purple, blue **Blooms:** spring
Hardiness: hardy

ONE OF THE MOST STRIKING USES OF THIS PLANT IS BETWEEN
flagstones set on sand. I used this technique when I was putting up a display
garden at the Alameda County Fair in Pleasanton. I built a large Arizona
Flagstone terrace and left planting space between all of the stones. I planted
False Rockcress along with the annual Sweet Alyssum and low-growing,
flowering perennials such as Candytuft and Moss Pink. Instead of a flat
rocky surface, the area became a flowering patio. The large stones provided
plenty of usable deck area.

Planting

Seeding: Direct sow in late spring; plants will likely not flower until the next year. Seeds collected from garden plants probably won't come true to type.

Transplanting: Fall

Spacing: 12–18"

Growing

False Rockcress prefers **full sun** but tolerates partial shade. The soil should be of **average fertility, moist** and **well drained,** with rocks or gravel mixed in. This plant also prefers soil to be a little on the alkaline side.

False Rockcress should be sheared back by half once it has finished flowering, to encourage compact growth and possibly a second flush of blooms later in the season. Every year or two, in fall, False Rockcress will need dividing in order to prevent the clump from thinning and dying out in the middle. New plants can be made from cuttings taken in summer. Shear the old flowers because seedlings will not bloom true to type.

Tips

Use False Rockcress in the crevices of a rock wall, between the paving stones of a pathway, in a rock garden, along the edge of a border or beneath taller plants.

Recommended

There are many cultivars, and their parentage is somewhat uncertain. Depending on the source, they are attributed to either *A. deltoidea* or *A.* x *cultorum*. All are low, mounding or cascading perennials that flower in early or mid-spring. Check with your local garden center for availability. '**Novalis Blue**' bears dark blue flowers and can be grown from seed. '**Purple Cascade**' bears purple flowers and is readily available. '**Variegata**' bears blue-purple flowers and has gold-variegated foliage.

Problems & Pests

Rare problems with aphids, nematodes or flea beetles can occur.

Fan Flower

Scaevola

Height: 4–30" **Spread:** 1–5' **Flower color:** blue, purple **Blooms:** year-round
Hardiness: semi-hardy

FAN FLOWERS HAVE USES IN EVERY GARDEN. THEIR CREEPING
habit means the plants can be used as groundcovers, as 'Mauve Clusters' is
often used in full-sun areas. They are also used in borders around roses and
other shrubs. I planted fan flowers with fleabane and achieved dynamite
effects, because neither of these plants is ever out of bloom. With the addition of bright red plants such as red geraniums, your window box will get
everyone's attention.

Scaevola *was named
for the Roman 'hero'
Mutius Scaevola, who
burned off his hand
to prove his bravery.*

Planting

Seeding: Indoors in late winter

Transplanting: February through July; from 4" pots

Spacing: 2–4'

Growing

Fan flowers grow well in **full sun** but tolerate afternoon shade. The soil should be of **average fertility, moist** and **well drained**. Water regularly, because these plants don't like to dry out completely. They do recover quickly from wilting when they are watered.

In the Sacramento Valley, fan flower plants will require more water during hot days. It is best to mulch around the plants with cedar bark or other sterile bark material.

Tips

Fan flowers are popular for hanging baskets and containers, but they can also be used along the tops of rock walls and in rock gardens where the plants can trail down. These plants look good in mixed borders or under shrubs, where the long, trailing stems form an attractive groundcover. Space at 24" when planting as a groundcover.

Recommended

S. aemula forms a mound of foliage from which trailing stems emerge. The height can reach 24–30" and the spread 3–4'. The fan-shaped flowers come in shades of purple, usually with white bases. The species is rarely grown because there are many improved cultivars. 'Blue Wonder' has long branches that

S. aemula (this page)

trail, making it ideal for hanging baskets. It can eventually spread 3' or more. 'Saphira' is a new, compact variety with deep blue flowers. It spreads 12" or more.

S. 'Mauve Clusters' is a mat-forming plant growing 4–6" tall and spreading 3–5'. Mauve flowers are produced for an extended period with a big flush of blooms in summer.

Problems & Pests

Whiteflies may cause problems for fan flower plants if they become stressed from lack of water.

Fleabane

Erigeron

Height: 12–24" **Spread:** 12–36" **Flower color:** white, pink, purple
Blooms: summer **Hardiness:** semi-hardy to hardy

FLEABANES CAN BE GROWN QUITE SUCCESSFULLY IN MOST OF
Northern California. In the hot interior valleys they require afternoon shade
to survive the heat. Because they so well adapted to coastal areas of California
and Oregon, they may become pests. In my mind, though, there aren't more
beautiful garden pests anywhere. As a bonus, these plants are deer resistant.

Planting

Seeding: Sow seeds into containers in cold frame in mid- to late spring

Transplanting: Fall

Spacing: 9–24"

Growing

Fleabanes grow in **full sun** or **light shade**. The soil should be **average to rich** and **well drained**. Even sandy soils will do, provided there is some organic matter well mixed in. The plants produce more flowers if the soil does not become excessively dry, and occasional supplemental watering during dry spells may be required. Divide these long-lived plants every two or three years in spring or fall to keep them vigorous. Discard the old woody growth when dividing. Deadhead fleabanes to encourage them to continue flowering.

The taller species require support to prevent them from flopping over. Twiggy branches pushed into the soil around the plants while they are small will provide support as the plants grow and will be hidden once the plants are fully grown.

Tips

Fleabanes are an excellent choice for the middle or front of a border. Low, mat-forming species are attractive in a rock garden, on a rock wall or in hanging baskets.

Recommended

E. glaucus (Beach Aster) is a sprawling plant about 12" tall and 18" wide. This species is native to the Pacific coast and is quite tolerant of salt spray. Keep it out of the hottest afternoon sun. Good cultivars are available with yellow-centered pink or white flowers.

E. karvinskianus (Santa Barbara Daisy) is a trailing plant growing 12–18" tall and spreading 24–36".

'White Quakeress'

The common name comes from a traditional use of these plants to keep rooms free of fleas.

The yellow-centered flowers have white petals that fade to pink, then red-purple. This plant tolerates drought once established.

E. speciosus (Oregon Fleabane) is another Pacific coast native. Many cultivars and hybrids have been developed from this species. They range from 12–24" in height and width. A few cultivars are **'Charity,'** with light pink flowers; **'Dignity,'** a smaller cultivar with deep pink flowers; and **'White Quakeress,'** with very pale, almost white flowers. All flower centers are yellow.

Problems & Pests

Downy and powdery mildew, rust, smut and leaf spot may cause occasional problems.

Foamflower
Tiarella

Height: 12–18" **Spread:** 18–24" **Flower color:** white, pink
Blooms: spring, sometimes to early summer **Hardiness:** hardy

FOAMFLOWERS ARE AMONG THE BEST PLANTS TO USE AS GROUND-covers around camellias and other shade-loving plants. Place a foamflower under and around David Viburnum for a knockout contrast in foliage color. Fern gardens will also benefit from an introduction of one of the varieties listed here.

Planting

Seeding: Start in cold frame in spring

Transplanting: Spring

Spacing: 18–24"

The starry flowers cluster along the long stems, looking like festive sparklers.

Growing

Foamflowers prefer **partial, light or full shade** protected from afternoon sun. The soil should be **humus rich, moist** and **slightly acidic**. These plants adapt to most soils. Divide in spring.

Deadhead to extend blooming. If the foliage fades or rusts in summer, cut it partway to the ground and fresh new growth will emerge.

Tips

Foamflowers make excellent ground-covers for shaded and woodland gardens. They can be included in shaded borders and left to naturalize in wild gardens.

These plants spread by underground rhizomes, which are easily pulled up to prevent excessive sprawl.

Recommended

T. cordifolia is a low-growing, spreading, evergreen perennial. This plant is attractive enough to be grown for the foliage alone, and cultivars with interesting variegation are becoming available. Spikes of foamy flowers are borne in spring. This plant is native to eastern North America. **'Filigree Lace'** has lobed leaves with lacy leaf edges and dark patches at the base of each leaf. The plants grow 12–18" tall and 18–24" wide and bear white to pink flowers.

T. **'Maple Leaf'** is a clump-forming hybrid with bronze-green, maple-like leaves and pink-flushed flowers.

T. **'Skeleton Key'** has white flowers and deeply cut foliage with dark purple midribs.

Problems & Pests

Rust, snails and slugs are possible problems.

T. 'Maple Leaf' (above), *T. cordifolia* (below)

Foxglove
Digitalis

Height: 3–5' **Spread:** 12–24"
Flower color: pink, white
Blooms: spring if planted in fall; fall if
planted in spring **Hardiness:** hardy

D. PURPUREA IS THE FOXGLOVE MOST
people are familiar with and was the mainstay
of my Grandma's garden. She grew it quite
well in her shade garden despite the heat. In
my nursery in Belvedere, which is now Bayside
Gardens, we sold a lot of plants in one-gallon
containers. Plants purchased in six-packs will
bloom the first year and will bloom again
on shorter stems if the first flowering spikes
are removed before they set seed. To have
plants for the next year, allow the second
set of flowering spikes to set seed.

Planting

Seeding: Direct sow or start in cold
frame in early spring. Flowers are
unlikely the first year.

Transplanting: Spring or fall;
from six-packs

Spacing: 18–24"

*The heart medication
digitalis is made from
extracts of foxglove.
For over 200 years,*
D. purpurea *has been
used for treating heart failure.*

Growing

Foxgloves prefer **partial to full shade**. The soil should be **fertile, humus rich, moist** and **acidic**. These plants adapt to most soils that are neither too wet nor too dry. Some staking may be required in a windy location. Remove the tallest spike and the side shoots will bloom on shorter stalks that may not need staking.

You may wish to deadhead foxgloves once they have finished flowering, but it is a good idea to leave some of the spikes in place to spread seeds. Division is unnecessary because these plants will not live long enough to be divided.

Tips

Foxgloves are a must for the cottage garden or for people interested in heritage plants. They make an excellent vertical accent along the back of a border and are an interesting addition to a woodland garden.

D. purpurea (this page), with plantain lily (below)

Foxgloves are extremely poisonous, and simply touching a plant has been known to cause rashes, headaches and nausea.

'Alba' (above)

If you have too many plants, you may wish to thin them out or transplant some to another location—perhaps into a friend's garden.

Recommended

D. purpurea (Common Foxglove) is usually treated as an annual or biennial. Its ability to self-seed makes the plant appear perennial. It forms a basal rosette of foliage from which tall flowering spikes emerge, growing 4–5' high and 24" wide. Flowers come in a range of colors and the insides of the flowers are often spotted with contrasting colors. **'Alba'** bears white flowers. **'Apricot'** bears apricot pink flowers. **Excelsior Hybrids** grow to 5' tall and are available in many colors. They bear dense spikes of flowers. **Foxy Hybrids,** which come in a range of colors, are

The hybrid varieties become less vigorous with time and self-sown seedlings may not come true to type. Sprinkle new seed in your foxglove bed each spring to ensure a steady show from the lovely flowers.

considered dwarf by foxglove standards but easily reach 3' in height.

Alternate Species

D. x *mertonensis* (Strawberry Foxglove) is a true perennial. It bears rose pink flowers and grows 3–4' tall and 12–18" wide. This is a wonderful plant for coastal gardens. It is used extensively in special public gardens such as the Elizabeth Gamble Gardens in Palo Alto.

Problems & Pests

Anthracnose, fungal leaf spot, powdery mildew, root rot, stem rot, aphids, Japanese beetles and mealybugs are possible problems for foxgloves. Good air circulation and morning watering help reduce any problems.

D. purpurea (this page)

Gaura

Gaura

Height: 2–4' **Spread:** 24–36" **Flower color:** white, pink **Blooms:** late spring or early summer until frost **Hardiness:** hardy

GAURA MAKES AN IDEAL PLANT FOR AREAS THAT ARE DIFFICULT to water. Partner it with other drought-resistant plants such as Mexican Sage, Cleveland Sage, and any of the wormwoods. When used with wormwood, Gaura brings an impressive height above the gray foliage. This combination is quite deer resistant.

Planting

Seeding: Plant in containers in cold frame in spring or early summer

Transplanting: Spring; available in one-gallon containers

Spacing: 24–36"

Growing

Gaura prefers a location in **full sun** but tolerates partial shade. The soil should be **fertile, moist** and **well drained**. The plant forms a deep taproot and is drought tolerant once established. Division is difficult because of the taproot. Propagate by softwood or basal cuttings in spring, by seed or by transplanting self-sown seedlings before they form the taproot.

In order to keep this plant flowering right up until the end of the season, it is important to deadhead. Remove the spent flower spikes as they fade to promote more blooms, prevent excessive self-seeding and keep the plant tidy.

Tips

Gaura makes a good addition for borders. Its color and appearance have a softening effect on brighter colors. Although it bears few flowers at a time, it blooms for the entire summer.

Recommended

G. lindheimeri (White Gaura) is a clump-forming plant growing 30"–4' tall and 24–36" wide. Clusters of star-shaped white flowers arise from pink flower buds. The flowers fade back to pink with age. **'Corrie's Gold'** is a compact plant, growing 24–30" tall, with gold variegation around the edges of its leaves. **'Siskiyou Pink'** grows to 24" tall. It bears bright pink flowers and its foliage is marked with reddish purple. **'Whirling Butterflies'** grows to 36" tall and tends to have more flowers in bloom at a time.

Problems & Pests

Generally pest free, Gaura may have occasional problems with gophers, rust, fungal leaf spot, downy mildew and powdery mildew.

Gayfeather

Blazing Star, Spike Gayfeather

Liatris

Height: 24–36" **Spread:** 18–24"
Flower color: purple, white **Blooms:** summer
Hardiness: hardy

GAYFEATHER ADDS A wonderful vertical accent to your garden. It is a very popular cut flower in florists' shops and should be added to your own cutting garden. You can find it in six-packs at specialty nurseries from February to April; otherwise, wait until May to June and purchase blooming plants in one-gallon containers. Gayfeather is also often available in bare-root form in spring. Check in catalogs that feature Dutch bulb growers to see what is available.

Planting

Seeding: Direct sow in fall; plants may take two to four years to bloom from seed

Transplanting: February to June

Spacing: 18–24"

Gayfeather will attract butterflies and hummingbirds to your garden.

Growing

Gayfeather prefers **full sun**. The soil should be of **average fertility, moist, well drained** and **humus rich**. Water well during the growing season, but don't allow the plant to stand in water during cool weather or over the winter; soggy soil may kill it. Mulch during the summer to prevent moisture loss. Divide every three or four years in early spring or when the plant is not performing well. The clump will appear crowded when it is time to divide.

Trim off the spent flower spikes to promote a longer blooming period and keep the plant looking tidy.

Tips

Use Gayfeather in beds, borders and meadow plantings. It grows well in planters. It also makes an excellent cut flower.

Good drainage is key. If you are unsure whether your area has sufficient drainage, lift the roots of your Gayfeather plant at the end of the season and store them in 10" fiber pots with slightly moist planting mix. Re-plant them in spring.

Recommended

L. spicata is an erect, clump-forming plant with pinkish purple or white flowers. **'Floristan Violet'** has purple flowers. **'Floristan White'** grows to 36" tall and has white flowers. **'Kobold'** is a compact plant, 24" tall, with deep purple flowers.

Problems & Pests

Slugs, stem rot, root rot, rust and leaf spot are possible problems.

'Floristan White' (above), 'Kobold' (below)

Geranium
Pelargonium

Height: 8–36" **Spread:** 6"–5' **Flower color:** red, pink, orange, salmon, white, purple **Blooms:** spring, summer; some to frost **Hardiness:** semi-hardy

ONE OF THE MOST DIFFICULT THINGS NURSERY STAFF HAVE TO DO is to explain the difference between *Geranium* species—known as hardy geraniums—and *Pelargonium* species—known, confusingly, as geraniums. Here is what I tell people. If the plant has ferny leaves and rather unassuming flowers, it is a *Geranium*. If it has glorious, multi-headed blooms in the bright colors of the rainbow, it is a *Pelargonium*. And if it has small flowers but wonderful-smelling leaves, it is also a *Pelargonium*. Of course, everything may be subject to change by the Royal Horticulture Society of Great Britain, which can't seem to leave any plant name alone.

The genus name Pelargonium *arises from the Greek word for 'stork,'* pelargos. *The fruit resembles a stork's bill.*

Planting

Seeding: Species are easy to start from seed in early fall or spring. Only certain hybrids and cultivars can be started from seed in containers in early fall or spring. Other hybrids and cultivars may not come true to type.

Transplanting: Spring or fall

Spacing: Zonal Geranium, about 12"; Ivy-leaved and scented geraniums, 24–36"

Growing

Geraniums prefer **full sun**. They tolerate partial shade but may not bloom as profusely. The soil should be **fertile, humus rich** and **well drained**. Division can be done in spring.

Deadheading is essential to keep geraniums blooming and looking neat. The flowerheads are attached to long stems that break off easily where they attach to the plant. Some gardeners prefer to snip off just the flowering ends in order to avoid potentially damaging the stems. I have always removed both blooms and stems, to avoid making the plant look like a bunch of dead sticks. Remove unsightly foliage to keep plants looking fresh.

Geraniums are slow to grow from seed, so purchasing plants may prove easier. However, if you would like to try starting your own from seed, start them indoors in early winter and cover them with clear plastic to maintain humidity until they germinate. Once the seedlings have three or four leaves, transplant

Scented geranium cultivar (above), 'Chocolate-Mint' (below)

them into individual 3–4" pots. Keep them in a bright location because they need lots of light to maintain compact shape.

Tips

Ivy-leaved Geranium is most often used in hanging baskets and containers to take advantage of its trailing habit, but it is also interesting when used as a bedding plant to form a bushy, spreading groundcover. Use Zonal Geranium in beds, borders and containers. Scented geraniums are great in a herb or kitchen garden or as edging at the front of beds and borders. Plant them where you can smell the aromatic foliage. They are a wonderful surprise as you brush against them on a rainy day.

P. zonale (above), *P. peltatum* (below)

Recommended

There are many cultivars and varieties available. The following species and varieties are some of the easier ones to start from seed. Many popular varieties can be propagated only from cuttings and must be purchased as plants.

P. peltatum (Ivy-leaved Geranium) grows 12–18" tall and 3–5' wide. Many colors are available. Plants in the **'Summer Showers'** series can be grown from seed although they are somewhat slow to flower. The flowers come in shades of white, pink, red and purple. **'Tornado'** series is very good for hanging baskets and containers. The plants are quite compact, and the flowers are either lilac or white. In frost-free areas they make a very colorful groundcover.

P. zonale (*P.* x *hortorum*) (Zonal Geranium) grows up to 24" tall and 12" wide. Dwarf varieties grow up to 8" tall and 6" wide. The flowers are red, pink, purple, orange or white. **'Orbit'** series has attractive, early-blooming, compact plants. The seed is often sold in a mixed packet, but some individual colors are available. **'Pinto'** series is available in all colors, and seed is generally sold by the color so you don't have to purchase a mixed packet and hope you like the colors you get.

The scented geraniums are a large and diverse group of shrubby species and hybrids whose leaves emit pleasant aromas when bruised or crushed. The following are a few popular selections. They are not usually available from seed but are generally grown from cuttings.

'Prince of Orange' (above), *P. zonale* cultivar (below)

Many scented geraniums are used for flavoring food and drink. They are often added to jellies and potpourri and can give dry flower arrangements an appealing fragrance. Only P. crispum *and its cultivars and hybrids should be avoided for food and drink purposes.*

P. capitatum (Rose Geranium, Wild Rose Geranium) has weakly trailing stems 12–36" tall and 18"–5' in spread. It bears mauve pink flowers in clusters in summer. This species is used to make geranium oil. Other rose-scented geraniums include *P.* x *asperum* and *P. graveolens*.

P. x *nervosum* (Lime Geranium) is a shrubby perennial that grows 24–36" tall and wide and bears small pink flowers. Its foliage has a strong lime aroma.

P. 'Prince of Orange' grows 12–24" tall and spreads 24–36" wide. The dense foliage emits the aroma of oranges.

P. quercifolium (Oak-leaf Geranium) is a shrubby perennial up to 36" tall and wide with purple-pink flowers in summer. The species has a spicy scent. 'Chocolate-Mint'

P. zonale with *Labularia* (above),
P. peltatum cultivars (below)

('Chocolate-Peppermint') is more compact than the species. Its velvet-textured leaves are marked with purple to brown. The aroma is somewhat minty with a hint of chocolate. **'Pretty Polly'** (Almond Geranium) has a strong, nutty, almond-like aroma.

P. tomentosum (Peppermint Geranium) is a trailing, evergreen perennial with velvet-textured foliage and a refreshing mint aroma. It grows 12–24" tall, spreads 18–36" and bears white flowers in spring and summer.

Problems & Pests

Aphids will flock to overfertilized plants, but they can usually be washed off before they do much damage. Other common pests include whiteflies and spider mites. Infrequent problems with bacterial blight, downy and powdery mildew, gray mold, leaf spot, leaf miners and slugs are possible.

Edema is an unusual condition to which geraniums are susceptible. This disease occurs when a plant is overwatered and the leaf cells burst, resulting in a warty surface on the leaves. There is no cure, although the problem can be avoided by watering carefully and by removing any damaged leaves as the plant grows. The condition is more common in Ivy-leaved Geranium.

P. peltatum with *Coleus* and *Helichrysum* (above), *P. zonale* (below)

Ivy-leaved Geranium is one of the most beautiful plants to include in a mixed hanging basket.

Geum
Avens
Geum

Height: 12–24" **Spread:** 12–24" **Flower color:** orange, red, yellow
Blooms: late spring, summer; sometimes also fall **Hardiness:** hardy

GEUMS, LIKE SHASTA DAISY AND MANY OTHER PERENNIALS WITH
fibrous roots, benefit from biannual digging and dividing. By doing so, you
can refresh the soil periodically with new planting mix and fertilizer, and you
will prevent the center of the plant from becoming so matted that the flowers don't bloom, *G. coccineum*, Scarlet Avens, makes an ideal addition to a
rock garden. It works well when planted between patio flagstones.

Planting

Seeding: Direct sow freshly ripened seeds
in fall or early spring

Transplanting: Spring or fall; from six-packs

Spacing: 12–24"

Growing

Geums prefer **full sun** but don't like excessive heat. The soil should be **fertile, evenly moist** and **well drained**. Geums do not like water-logged soil. Geums like cool roots, so provide a layer of mulch. Divide every year or two in spring or fall. Cut off spent flowers to keep more coming.

Tips

Geums make a bright-flowered addition to the border. They look particularly attractive combined with plants that have dark blue or purple flowers.

Recommended

G. coccineum (Scarlet Avens) forms a mounded clump. Scarlet red flowers are borne from late spring to late summer. '**Borisii**' is a compact, neat plant 12" tall and wide with bright orange single flowers. It often re-blooms in the fall. '**Fire Lake**' grows to 12" tall and produces orange-red flowers in late spring to early summer. '**Prince of Orange**' bears bright orange flowers until mid-summer on plants 20–24" tall and wide.

G. quellyon (*G. chiloense*) (Chilean Avens) is a clump-forming plant 16–24" tall, with an equal spread. It bears bright scarlet flowers all summer. '**Fire Opal**' bears semi-double orange-red flowers and is slightly taller than the species. '**Lady Stratheden**' has bright yellow semi-double flowers. '**Mrs. Bradshaw**' bears dark red-orange semi-double flowers.

G. quellyon with *Euphorbia polychroma* (right)

'Lady Stratheden' (above)

Problems & Pests

Geums have problems with downy mildew, powdery mildew, fungal leaf spot and leaf smut. Water in the morning only. Caterpillars may occasionally cause trouble.

Globe Thistle
Echinops

Height: 6"–5' **Spread:** 6–30" **Flower color:** shades of blue
Blooms: mid-summer to late fall **Hardiness:** hardy

GLOBE THISTLES ARE VERY EASY TO GROW, REQUIRING MINIMAL
care. They thrive on neglect and produce an abundance of blooms from
mid-summer to mid-November. They can stay undivided for up to seven
years without losing their ability to produce copious amounts of flowers.
The unusual steel blue flowers make a great addition to
dry and fresh floral arrangements.

Planting

Seeding: Sow seed in flats or direct sow in
spring. Plants from seed are often inferior
to plants taken from divisions or root cuttings.

Transplanting: July to August; from one-
gallon containers

Spacing: 18–36"

*Globe thistles will attract butterflies
and bees to your garden.*

Growing

Globe thistles prefer **full sun** but tolerate partial shade. These plants will grow in most **well-drained** soils. A rich, fertile soil may cause excessive growth that requires staking. The plants are frost hardy and will tolerate heat and drought once established.

Cut to the ground in late fall, and divide every three to four years. Propagate by root cuttings or division in spring or fall.

Tips

Globe thistles are best used in a mixed perennial border or large, wild garden. The bright blue flowers look lovely against a dark green background.

The blooms make excellent cut flowers that retain their color if they are cut just as they open. Globe thistle flowers also work well for dried arrangements.

Recommended

All species listed here form upright clumps of spiny foliage.

E. bannaticus grows 18"–4' tall and 18–24" wide. It has blue to gray-blue flowers. 'Taplow Blue' is slightly taller than the species and bears striking, bright blue flowers.

E. exaltatus grows 3–5' tall, spreads 18–24" and has steel blue flowers.

E. humulis is a compact plant 6–12" tall and 6–9" wide, with steel blue flowers.

E. ritro (Small Globe Thistle) grows 24–36" tall and 16–30" wide. It has purple-blue to bright blue flowers.

Problems & Pests

Aphids may be a problem.

E. ritro (this page)

Golden Marguerite
Marguerite Daisy
Anthemis

Height: 24–36" **Spread:** 24–36" **Flower color:** yellow, orange, cream
Blooms: summer to early fall **Hardiness:** hardy

THIS MEMBER OF THE DAISY FAMILY CREATES A MASS OF YELLOW
flowers that cover the entire plant. The flowers hold up well in arrangements,
and the bold yellow color easily mixes with many flowering perennials in the
garden. The plant is short-lived and will need grooming after every bloom
cycle to continue flowering. This cousin of Chamomile has the same wonderful foliage fragrance that makes Chamomile tea so popular.

Planting
Seeding: Direct sow in spring

Transplanting: Spring

Spacing: 18–24"

Growing

Golden Marguerite prefers **full sun.**
The soil should be of **average fertility** and **well drained.** This plant can
handle periods of drought once
established, but watering once a
week is best. The clumps die out in
the middle and should be divided
every two or three years in spring or
fall. You can also propagate by stem
cuttings taken in spring or fall.

Golden Marguerite tends to flower
in waves. Cutting off the dead flowers will encourage continual flowering all summer. If the plant begins
to look thin and spread out, cut it
back hard to promote new growth
and flowers.

Tips

Golden Marguerite forms attractive
clumps with profuse blooms, and it
blends wonderfully into a cottage-
style garden. Its drought tolerance
makes it an ideal plant for rock gardens and exposed slopes. The
blooms make excellent cut flowers.

To avoid the need for staking, group
several plants together so they can
support each other.

Recommended

A. tinctoria forms a mounded
clump of foliage that is completely
covered with bright or creamy yellow, daisy-like flowers in summer
and early fall. '**Beauty of Grallach**'
has deep orange-yellow flowers.
'**E.C. Buxton**' has flowers with
creamy petals and yellow centers.
'**Grallach Gold**' has bright yellow-
gold flowers. '**Moonlight**' has large,
pale yellow flowers.

Problems & Pests

Golden Marguerite may suffer from
such fungal problems as powdery
or downy mildew, but only rarely.
Aphids can be a nuisance.

Gunnera
Giant Rhubarb
Gunnera

Height: 6–8' **Spread:** 10–12' **Flower color:** reddish green, rust red
Blooms: summer **Hardiness:** semi-hardy

THESE ARE PLANTS THAT CRY FOR SPACE. I SAW ONE ONCE THAT was so large you could walk under it. I used a gunnera in a display garden in the Sonoma County Fair, as a dramatic accent surrounded by Transvaal Daisy. The contrast of bold foliage with the daisy was spectacular. Unfortunately, the judges didn't know what the plant was and deducted points from my score. I won 'Best Design' anyway, though the loss of points did cost me 'Best in Show.' I have been leery of judges ever since.

Planting

Seeding: Direct sow ripe seed in fall; can be slow to germinate

Transplanting: Spring

Spacing: 10'

Growing

Gunneras can be grown in **full sun** to **partial shade**. Keep them out of the hottest afternoon sun to avoid leaf scorch; they suffer in a combination of high heat and humidity. Shelter from cold, drying or strong winds. The soil should be **humus rich, fertile** and **constantly moist**. These plants like to be fed and watered regularly.

Protect the crown of your gunnera in winter with a thick layer of dry mulch.

Grow from seed or from cuttings of the basal leaf buds in spring.

Tips

Gunneras are bold, striking plants with extremely large leaves. They are best used as accent or feature plants near a pond or in a bog garden. They can also be used in beds if given plenty of water and space.

Recommended

G. manicata forms large clumps 8' high and 10–12' or more wide. Each large, deeply veined, lobed leaf blade is 4–8' wide, at the end of a 4–8' leaf stalk. Branches of tiny, green-red flowers appear in early summer on 36" long, somewhat conical spikes that resemble bottlebrushes. Rounded, green-red fruits follow.

G. tinctoria (*G. chilensis*) forms clumps slightly smaller than those of *G. manicata*. The leaf blades are 3–6' wide on stalks 5' long. They are more deeply lobed than those of *G. manicata*. Branches of tiny, rust red flowers are produced on 20–24" cylindrical spikes in early to late summer, followed by round, green-red fruit.

Problems & Pests

Slugs and snails are problems.

Gunnera leaves are among the largest of all broad-leaved plants.

G. manicata (this page)

Hellebore

Helleborus

Height: 12–18" **Spread:** 12–18" **Flower color:** white, green, pink, purple, cream **Blooms:** early winter to spring **Hardiness:** hardy

HELLEBORES ARE WINNERS IN GARDENS WHERE BOLD FOLIAGE is needed. Take care when buying these plants, as they are often mislabeled. Christmas Rose has lustrous, dark green leaves. It absolutely needs afternoon shade, but morning sun is fine in the cooler climates of the northern parts of the state. Lenten Rose has deep green leaves and will self-sow freely. It is more heat tolerant than Christmas Rose and will flourish in coastal areas in full sun but needs afternoon shade in the hot interior valleys. Many growers sell these plants in one-gallon containers. I prefer plants available in larger containers; they cost more but give a better idea of what you are buying.

Planting

Seeding: Not recommended; seed is very slow to germinate

Transplanting: Spring or late summer

Spacing: 12–18"

Growing

Hellebores prefer **light, dappled shade** to **full shade** in a sheltered site. The soil should be **fertile, moist, humus rich, neutral to alkaline** and **well drained**. Division is not recommended; these plants do not like to have their roots disturbed.

Allow hellebores to self-sow. The seedlings can be transplanted to increase your plant population. They will crossbreed with other varieties, and you may wish to select different hybrids with unusual foliage.

Tips

Use these plants in a sheltered border or rock garden or naturalize in a woodland garden. When planted near a path or an entrance, the blooms can brighten a late-winter day.

Recommended

H. niger (Christmas Rose) is a clump-forming evergreen that blooms from early winter to spring. The flowers are white fading to pink. This plant should be in shade and the soil must be a little alkaline for the best performance. 'Potter's Wheel' bears large white flowers with green centers. 'White Magic' has large white blooms.

H. orientalis (Lenten Rose) is a variable, clump-forming, evergreen perennial. In late winter to spring, it bears flowers in shades of white, pink, purple, cream or green.

Problems & Pests

Slugs, aphids, crown rot, leaf spot or black rot can be problems.

H. niger (above), *H. orientalis* (below)

Hens and Chicks
Roof Houseleek
Sempervivum

Height: 3–6" **Spread:** 12" to indefinite **Flower color:** pinkish red, purple-red; plant grown for foliage **Blooms:** summer **Hardiness:** hardy

HENS AND CHICKS ARE EASY TO GROW AND PROPAGATE. EACH mother rosette gathers her chicks around her base. As these little wonders are separated from the mother, they then produce their own colony of little chicks. I have seen these plants growing abundantly along the coast, wedged into crevasses of rock walls anywhere there is space to send down roots. It is easy to have the same effect in your own garden.

Admired for the thick, waxy foliage, these plants produce many 'chicks' that can be easily transplanted. Placed in a small amount of dirt between the stones of a rock wall, hens and chicks will look right at home.

Planting

Seeding: Seeds may be started in cold frame in spring

Transplanting: Spring

Spacing: 10–12"

Growing

Hens and chicks can grow in **full sun** or **partial shade**. They appreciate some shade from the hottest afternoon sun. The soil should be **poor to average** and very **well drained**. Add fine gravel or grit to the soil to provide adequate drainage.

Once a plant blooms, it dies. When you deadhead the faded flower, pull up the soft parent plant as well to provide space for the new daughter rosettes that sprout up, seemingly by magic. Divide by removing new rosettes and rooting them.

S. tectorum (this page)

S. tectorum (this page)

Tips

These plants make excellent additions to rock gardens and rock walls, where they will even grow right on the rocks.

The biggest challenge in growing these plants is preventing them from getting too wet in winter. If you don't have a well-drained location in the garden, grow them under an overhang of the house or in clay containers that can be moved to a sheltered spot in winter. The hairy-leaved species are more likely to be killed by too much moisture.

You can grow these plants on the outside of a wire frame lined with green moss. Attach plants with wire to make interesting patterns. Use a hand sprayer to water.

Recommended

S. tectorum forms a low-growing mat of fleshy-leaved rosettes. Each rosette is 3–6" across, but it quickly produces new rosettes that will fill almost any space. Purple-red flowers are produced in summer but are not showy. **'Atropurpureum'** has dark reddish purple leaves. **'Limelight'** has yellow-green, pink-tipped foliage. **'Pacific Hawk'** has dark red leaves edged with silvery hairs.

Hens and chicks can grow on almost any surface—in the past these plants were grown on tile roofs, and it was believed they would protect the house from lightning.

Alternate Species

S. arachnoideum (Cobweb House-leek) has smaller individual rosettes than *S. tectorum*. Its leaves are tipped with hairy fibers, giving the appearance of cobwebs. The flowers are pinkish red and are borne in summer.

S. ciliosum has very hairy, gray-green succulent leaves on rosettes 2–3" wide. It bears flattened clusters of greenish yellow flowers in summer.

Problems & Pests

Hens and chicks plants are generally pest free, although some problems with rust and root rot can occur.

The juice from the leaves can be applied to burns, insect bites and other skin irritations.

S. tectorum (this page)

Hibiscus

Rose-Mallow

Hibiscus

Height: 18"–8' **Spread:** 36" **Flower color:** white, red, pink
Blooms: early summer to frost **Hardiness:** hardy

HIBISCUS PLANTS ARE EXCEPTIONALLY TOUGH AND VERSATILE, surviving summer heat as well as temperatures to –25° F. They are drought resistant once established but also tolerate wet feet as long as there is plenty of organic matter added to the soil. With their large blooms and long blooming cycle, hibiscus plants make beautiful specimen plants or centerpieces of a perennial bed.

Planting

Seeding: Sow seeds in spring when soil temperature is 55–64° F

Transplanting: Spring

Spacing: 36"

Growing

Grow hibiscus plants in **full sun.** The soil should be **humus rich, moist** and **well drained.** Plant in a site sheltered from the wind. Divide in spring.

Deadhead to keep the plants tidy. Prune plants by one-half in June for bushier, more compact growth. Pinch plants when they are 8" tall and again when they reach 3'. If you purchase them in containers, pinching will already have been done.

H. moscheutos cultivar

Moisture-loving hibiscus plants are very exotic-looking plants to include in a bog garden or pond-side planting.

'Southern Belle'

Tips

These plants are interesting at the back of an informal border or mixed into a pond planting. The large flowers, often the size of dinner plates, create a bold focal point and make a very colorful addition to late-summer gardens. The plants can also be used as a summertime hedge.

Recommended

H. moscheutos is a large, vigorous plant with strong stems. It grows 6–8' tall and 36" wide. The huge flowers—up to 12" across—come in shades of red, pink and white. The following selections are propagated by cuttings. **'Blue River II'** grows about 4' tall and bears pure

'Blue River II'

white flowers. '**Lady Baltimore**' grows to 4' and has red-centered, glowing pink flowers. '**Lord Baltimore**' bears ruffled, bright red flowers. It also reaches a height of 4'.

Gilberg Hybrids, over 120 wonderful hybrids with blooms of many different colors and sizes, have been created by the people at Gilberg Farms. Check out their website at <www.hibiscuscentral.com>. You can order the hybrids through the website.

The following selections can be grown from seed. '**Disco Belle**' is a small plant 18–24" tall. It is often grown as an annual, and its flowers can be red, pink or white. '**Southern Belle**' bears red, pink or white flowers on large plants 4–6' tall.

Problems & Pests

Hibiscus plants are generally problem free but may develop problems with rust, fungal leaf spot, bacterial blight, *Verticillium* wilt, viruses and stem or root rot. A few possible insect pests are whiteflies, aphids, scale insects, mites and caterpillars.

Although hibiscus plants can come with light blue flowers, don't confuse these with their cousin, the so-called Blue Hibiscus, Alyogyne huegelii, *which is a shrub.*

Himalayan Poppy

Meconopsis

Height: 1–4' **Spread:** 12–24" **Flower color:** blue, yellow, orange, mauve
Blooms: late spring, summer, fall **Hardiness:** hardy to semi-hardy

I DON'T BELIEVE THERE IS A BETTER BLUE FLOWER TO GROW IN shade beds than *M. betonicifolia*, Himalayan Poppy. The plants of this species tend to do best when the weather is cool. They are not recommended for the hot interior valleys except in areas such as Willits where the winters are cool enough to keep the plants growing. For many areas of Northern California, *M. cambrica*, Welsh Poppy, might be a better selection. It is more heat tolerant if given afternoon shade but does not bear the magnificent blue blooms of Himalayan Poppy.

Planting

Seeding: Sow seed when ripe or in spring; do not cover seeds because they need light to germinate

Transplanting: Spring

Spacing: 12–24"

Growing

Himalayan poppies prefer to grow in **partial to full shade** in **moist, well-drained, humus-rich, neutral to acidic** soil. Provide shelter from cold, drying winds, especially on the coast, and hot afternoon sun. These plants prefer cool, humid conditions. Ensure you supply adequate water. Propagate by seed or by division after flowering. Keep the soil moist but not wet when the seeds are germinating.

In California you will probably have to grow these plants from seed as they are not usually commercially available as plants.

Tips

Himalayan poppies are best used in a woodland garden but can be grown in beds and borders as long as their cultural requirements are met. *M. cambrica* has a taproot and can handle some drought and sun in cool summer areas. It is also less particular than *M. betonicifolia* when it comes to soil preferences. *Meconopsis* plants will self-seed but are not very invasive.

Recommended

*M. **betonicifolia*** (Himalayan Poppy) forms rosettes of hairy foliage. It can reach a height of up to 4' under ideal conditions. It spreads 18–24". Blue flowers with yellow stamens are borne from late spring to early summer. In less than ideal conditions, Himalayan Poppy will be a smaller plant with flowers in mauve instead of blue.

M. betonicifolia (above), *M. cambrica* (below)

M. cambrica (Welsh Poppy) is an erect plant with basal tufts of foliage and branched stems. It grows 12–24" tall and 12" wide and bears yellow flowers from late spring to fall. It self-seeds profusely. '**Aurantiaca**' (var. *aurantiaca*) produces orange flowers. '**Flore Pleno**' bears yellow or orange double flowers.

Problems & Pests

Slugs, snails and damping off may cause problems.

Iris

Iris

Height: 6"–4' **Spread:** 6"–4' **Flower color:** many shades of pink, red,
purple, blue, white, brown, yellow **Blooms:** spring, summer
Hardiness: hardy to semi-hardy

AUGUST IS THE MAGIC MONTH FOR WORKING WITH IRISES IN
Northern California. This is the time to cut back, divide or mulch. *Iris germanica* needs re-planting every three years, but other iris species are not so
fussy. When planting irises, select specimens with different blooming times
to have flowers as long as possible. In my garden the blooms start in late February and extend to the end of June. All irises are stunning and long lasting
in flower arrangements, and all are deer resistant.

Planting

Seeding: Seeds may be started in containers in a cold frame in fall. They may not bloom the first year from seed.

Transplanting: September from bare-root stock; year round from one-gallon containers

Spacing: 2"–4'

Growing

Irises prefer to grow in **full sun** but tolerate very light or dappled shade. The soil should be **average** or **fertile** and **well drained**. Siberian Iris prefers a moist, well-drained soil. Divide in late summer or early fall.

Tips

Irises are popular border plants, but some species are also useful beside streams or ponds, and others make attractive additions to rock gardens.

Irises are depicted on the wall of an Egyptian temple dating from 1500 BC, making them among the oldest cultivated plants.

Their appealing scent and colors make iris blooms popular additions to potpourri.

Pacific Coast Hybrids

I. douglasiana (above), *I. germanica* (below)

It is a good idea to wash your hands after handling these plants because they can cause severe internal irritation if ingested. Make sure they are not planted close to places where children play.

Recommended

Hundreds of different iris species and cultivars are available, to suit almost any garden situation. The following is a very short list of irises appropriate for our climate. Visiting a local garden center or specialty grower (there are several iris growers in Northern California) will give you a good idea of what is available.

I. douglasiana (Douglas Iris) is native to the Pacific Northwest and is well suited to the conditions of our region. It grows 6–28" tall and flowers from March through June. Many colors are available. This iris does best when not irrigated throughout the summer.

I. germanica (Bearded Iris) has flowers in all colors. This iris has been used as the parent for many desirable cultivars. Cultivars may vary in height and width from 6" to 4'. Flowering ranges from mid-spring to mid-summer, and some cultivars flower again in fall.

Pacific Coast Hybrids are popular cultivars developed mostly from crosses between *I. douglasiana* and *I. innominata*. Many colors and sizes are available.

I. sibirica (Siberian Iris) is more resistant to iris borers than other species. This species grows 2–4' tall and 36" wide, and it flowers in early summer. Cultivars are available with flowers in many shades, mostly purple, blue and white.

I. unguicularis (Algerian Iris, Winter Iris) provides color to winter gardens with flowers in shades of purple. The plant grows about 12" tall. It flowers in late winter, early spring and sometimes in late fall.

Problems & Pests

Several problems tend to plague irises. Close observation will prevent these problems from becoming severe. Iris borers can be lethal. They burrow their way down the leaf until they reach the root, where they continue eating until no root is left. The tunnels they make in the leaves are easy to spot, and if infected leaves are removed and destroyed or the borers squished within them, the borers will never reach the roots.

Leaf spot is another problem that can be controlled by removing and destroying infected leaves. Be sure to give the plants the correct growing conditions. For some species too much moisture will allow rot diseases to settle in and kill the plants. A strong application of lime-sulfur spray prior to bloom will prevent most fungal problems. Slugs, snails, thrips and aphids may also cause some trouble.

Iris is the name of the Greek goddess of the rainbow. The name refers to the flowers' variable colors.

Pacific Coast Hybrid (center)

I. germanica (below)

Jacob's Ladder

Polemonium

Height: 8–36" **Spread:** 8–18" **Flower color:** blue, purple, white
Blooms: spring to early summer **Hardiness:** hardy

BLUE CAN BE A DIFFICULT COLOR TO COME BY IN THE GARDEN.
Jacob's ladder plants are among the best for providing that color. These
plants got their name because of the arrangement of the leaves. The leaves
form a sort of a ladder that could be used as such
if Heaven were closer and Jacob were smaller.

Planting

Seeding: Start seed in spring or fall;
soil temperature 70° F. Seed can take
up to a month to germinate.

Transplanting: March through summer; from 4" pots

Spacing: 12"

*In ancient Greece, P. caeruleum
was mixed with wine and used
for treating dysentery, toothache
and poisonous bites. Later in
Europe it was used to treat rabies
and syphilis.*

Growing

Jacob's ladder species grow well in **partial to full shade**. The leaves can scorch in hot afternoon sun. In the Central Valley, make sure to provide afternoon shade. Along the coast, these plants can tolerate full sun. The soil should be **fertile, humus rich, moist** and **well drained**. Division is rarely required but should be done in spring or after flowering if desired. This plant self-seeds readily.

Deadhead regularly to prolong blooming.

'Brise d'Anjou' (below)

Tips

Include *P. caeruleum* in borders and woodland gardens. It is effective when grown in planters and can be a tall focal point in the center of a large urn or barrel. *P. reptans* can be used in rock gardens and to edge paths. It also works well as a container plant.

Recommended

P. caeruleum (Jacob's Ladder) forms a dense clump of basal foliage. Leafy upright stems are topped with clusters of purple flowers. This plant grows 18–36" tall and spreads about 12–18". Var. *album* has white flowers. **'Apricot Delight'** produces many mauve flowers with apricot pink centers. **'Brise d'Anjou'** has creamy white leaflet margins but does not bear as many flowers as the species.

P. reptans (Creeping Jacob's Ladder) is a low, mounding perennial 8–16" tall and equally wide. It bears small blue or lilac flowers in late spring and early summer. **'Blue Pearl'** is the most readily available variety.

Problems & Pests

These plants are generally pest free but occasionally can be afflicted with powdery mildew, leaf spot and rust.

Lady's Mantle
Alchemilla

Height: 3–18" **Spread:** up to 24" **Flower color:** yellow, yellowish green
Blooms: summer, early fall **Hardiness:** hardy

WITH THEIR PALE GREEN FOLIAGE, LADY'S MANTLE PLANTS CAN add a refined look to a fern garden or offer a good contrast to beds suffering from the brightness of impatiens. They are ideal as a groundcover next to fences or walls or under shade-loving plants. I like to use these plants as a groundcover or accent in areas that many other plants don't do well in because of insufficient sun.

Planting

Seeding: Direct sow fresh seed or start in containers in spring; transplant into garden while seedlings are small

Transplanting: Spring

Spacing: 24"

The fresh or dried flowers can be added to arrangements, and the leaves can be boiled to make a green dye for wool.

Growing

Lady's mantle plants grow best in **light shade** or **partial shade,** with protection from the afternoon sun. The soil should be **fertile, humus rich, moist** and **well drained.** These plants are drought resistant once established, but they dislike hot sun. Division is rarely required but can be done in spring or fall.

If your lady's mantle begins to look tired and heat-stressed in summer, trim it back so new foliage can fill in. If you want more plants use some of the self-seeded plants that are bound to show up.

A. alpina (above), *A. mollis* (below)

Tips

These plants are ideal for grouping under trees in woodland gardens and along border edges, where the lady's mantle will soften the bright colors of other plants. A wonderful location is along a pathway that winds through a lightly wooded area.

Lady's mantle plants thrive as groundcovers under shade-loving plants. The roots will not compete with those of azaleas, camellias and rhododendrons, and they tolerate the same fertilizers as those shrubs. Lady's mantles are especially effective in standard gardens.

Recommended

A. alpina (Alpine Lady's Mantle) is a low-growing plant 3–5" tall and up to 20" in spread. It has soft white hairs on the backs of the leaves, giving the appearance of a silvery margin around each leaf. Clusters of tiny yellow flowers are borne in summer.

A. mollis (Common Lady's Mantle) is the most frequently grown species. It forms a mound of soft, rounded foliage 8–18" tall and up to about 24" in spread. Sprays of yellowish green flowers held above the foliage may be borne from early summer to early fall.

Lamb's Ears
Woolly Betony
Stachys

Height: 6–18" **Spread:** 18–24"
Flower color: pink, purple; plant grown mainly for foliage
Blooms: late spring to summer
Hardiness: hardy

THIS LOVELY PLANT IS IDEAL AS an edging around flowerbeds next to driveways and sidewalks. It will contain the soil in the bed once established and prevent soil wash into unwanted areas. People constantly on the go should select cultivars that rarely produce flowers, such as 'Silver Carpet.' This cultivar makes a wonderful, carefree groundcover, which is something I really appreciate.

Stachys is the Greek word for 'spike.' The genus is named for the spike-like flower clusters.

Planting

Seeding: Direct sow or start in containers in cold frame in spring

Transplanting: February to November; from six-packs

Spacing: 18–24"

Growing

Lamb's Ears grows best in **full sun.** The soil should be of **poor or average fertility** and **well drained**. The leaves can rot in humid weather or if the soil is poorly drained. Prolonged rain or frost can also damage the leaves but the plant will recover. When the center of an older plant looks ratty, it is time to dig it up and divide it. Division can also be done in spring to yield more plants.

Remove spent flower spikes to keep the plant looking neat. Some gardeners remove all flower spikes and use Lamb's Ears strictly for its foliage. Select a flowerless cultivar if you don't want to deadhead.

Tips

Lamb's Ears makes a great groundcover in a new garden where the soil has not yet been amended. This low-maintenance plant will do well as long as good drainage is provided. It can be used to edge borders and pathways, providing a soft, silvery backdrop for vibrant colors in the border.

Recommended

S. byzantina (S. lanata) forms a mat of thick, woolly rosettes of leaves. Pinkish purple flowers are borne on stems held above the foliage. '**Big Ears**' has purple leaves that are

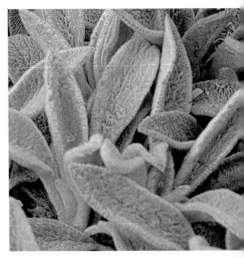

twice as big as those of the species. '**Silver Carpet**' has silvery white, fuzzy foliage; it rarely, if ever, produces flowers.

Problems & Pests

Fungal leaf problems, including rot, powdery mildew, rust and leaf spot, are rare but can occur in hot, humid weather. Cut back diseased or damaged foliage. New foliage will sprout when the weather cools.

Lantana
Shrub Verbena
Lantana

Height: 1–6' **Spread:** 1–8' **Flower color:** yellow, orange, red, pink, purple, cream, white **Blooms:** late spring to late summer
Hardiness: semi-hardy to tender

FEW PERENNIALS ARE MORE COLORFUL THAN LANTANAS, WHICH deserve to be used more often. They do best in hot locations and have low water requirements. I remember seeing a lantana long ago in San Francisco. In my child's eye, it was all yellows and reds and was inhabited by orange spiders that seemed to stare back at me! Mrs. Costa, my babysitter, explained to me that the spiders stole their faces from the plants, but my parents never believed me when I insisted I'd seen spiders with faces.

Planting

Seeding: Direct sow seed in spring when soil temperature reaches 61° F or indoors earlier

Transplanting: After last frost

Spacing: 3–5'

Growing

Lantanas prefer to grow in **full sun** in **fertile, moist, well-drained** soil. Overfertilizing and overwatering reduce flowering. These plants tolerate a light frost.

Propagate by softwood cuttings in summer or by seed. Seeding is not necessary because these plants are readily available in nurseries. Many people prefer to buy lantanas in bloom to get the color they want.

Lantanas bloom on new wood. To keep these plants looking good, cut back heavily in March after all danger of frost has passed.

Tips

The upright, shrubby lantanas are good for low hedges and for mixed beds. The trailing forms are useful for groundcovers, hanging baskets, walls and planters. *L. montevidensis* can form dense mats and makes an excellent groundcover that is effective for erosion control. Keep the spacing at 36" when using as a groundcover.

Recommended

L. camara (Yellow Sage) is an upright, rounded, often prickly shrub with aromatic foliage. It grows 3–6' tall and wide and bears orange to orange-yellow flowers

'Spreading Sunset' (above), 'White Lightnin'' (below)

Wear gloves when handling lantanas. The stems are often prickly and the foliage may irritate exposed skin.

'Spreading Sunset' (above),
'White Lightnin'' (below)

that fade to red or white. *L. camara* is a parent of many cultivars. Some of the cultivars listed here have *L. montevidensis* as the other parent. **'Confetti'** grows 24–36" tall and spreads 6–8'. It bears flowers in purple, pink and yellow. **'Cream Carpet'** grows 12–36" tall, spreads 3–6' and bears creamy white flowers with yellow throats. **'Radiation'** is a rounded form growing 3–5' tall with an equal spread. It produces golden orange and red flowers. **'Rainbow'** is a compact plant growing 12" tall and slightly wider. Its flowers come in yellow, orange and bright pink. **'Snow White'** grows 3–5' tall and wide and bears white flowers. **'Spreading Sunset'** reaches a height of 24–36" and spreads 6–8'. It bears bright orange-yellow flowers that fade to orange-red with age. **'Tangerine'** grows 24–36" tall, spreads 6–8' and bears orange blooms. **'Varia'** (forma *varia*) grows 3–5' tall and wide and has yellow flowers that turn purple on the outside and orange on the inside.

Florists use selections of L. camara *as cut flowers.*

The crushed leaves emit an interesting aroma that is not to everyone's liking.

L. montevidensis (L. delicatissima, L. sellowiana) (Weeping Lantana) is a weak-stemmed, trailing shrub growing 18–30" tall and spreading 3–6'. Small clusters of yellow-centered, rosy lilac to white flowers bloom for an extended period in summer. This species is the most frost hardy and deer proof of all lantanas. 'White Lightnin'' bears white flowers.

Problems & Pests

Lantanas have occasional problems with whiteflies, spider mites, rust, root-knot nematodes, stem rot, leaf spot and viral disease. They suffer from mildew in shade or during prolonged overcast periods.

'Spreading Sunset'

Lavender Cotton
Santolina

Height: 12–30" **Spread:** 16–36" **Flower color:** yellow, cream
Blooms: summer **Hardiness:** hardy

THESE ARE WONDERFUL PLANTS. SOME GARDENERS LIKE TO SHEAR the flower buds off so that the plant doesn't bloom. This technique keeps the plant looking solid without any dead wood showing. When cut back to ground level, *S. pinniata* will come back as a compact shrublet without any further care. It is used as a small hedge along with Japanese Barberry in the herb knot garden in the Filoli Center in Woodside. There are many uses of lavender cotton plants in low-maintenance gardens.

Planting

Seeding: Sow seed in spring or fall in cold frame

Transplanting: Spring

Spacing: 12"

Growing

Lavender cotton plants like **full sun** and **well-drained** soil of **poor to average fertility**. They are somewhat drought tolerant when established. Cut the plants back in spring before any new growth begins. Lightly shear off the faded flowerheads. Propagate by seed, by semi-hardwood cuttings in summer or by tip cuttings in fall.

Tips

Lavender cotton plants are nice for a rock garden, a low formal or informal hedge or a flowerbed. They are also useful as a groundcover and for erosion control. Try them as edging along a walkway, where the pleasing fragrance released by brushing or bruising the plant can be enjoyed.

Recommended

S. chamaecyparissus is an aromatic evergreen shrub with finely dissected white-gray foliage and bright yellow, button-like flowers. It grows 18–24" tall and 36" wide. '**Lemon Queen**' grows 24" tall with an equal spread. It bears pale to lemon yellow flowers. '**Nana**' grows to 12" tall and 24–36" wide. '**Pretty Carol**' is a compact plant growing 16" tall and wide.

S. pinniata grows 24–30" tall and 36" wide with dark green foliage and cream flowers.

The dry hillsides of the Mediterranean are the natural habitat of these tough and drought-resistant plants.

S. chamaecyparissus (this page)

Ligularia
Groundsel
Ligularia

Height: 3–6' **Spread:** 2–5'
Flower color: yellow, orange;
also grown for foliage
Blooms: summer, early fall
Hardiness: hardy

IN THE WARMER PARTS OF
Northern California, these plants
are best kept to moist areas in the
shade. To tolerate the heat they
also need good drainage.
The foliage is tremen-
dously attractive and
combines well with
coral bells, columbine
and other shade-loving,
low-growing perennials.

Planting

Seeding: Species can be
started outdoors in spring
in containers; cultivars
rarely come true to type
from seed

Transplanting: March
through July; from
one-gallon containers

Spacing: 2–5'

The name Ligularia *is derived
from the Latin word* ligula,
*which means 'a strap,' a reference
to the strap-shaped petals.*

Growing

Ligularias prefer **partial to full shade** with protection from afternoon sun. The soil should be **fertile, humus rich** and **moist**. These plants do not like low humidity or excess heat. Division is rarely required but can be done in spring or fall to propagate a desirable cultivar.

Tips

Use ligularias alongside a pond or stream. They can also be used in a well-watered border or naturalized in a moist meadow or woodland garden.

The foliage can wilt in hot sun, even in moist soil. The leaves will revive at night, but this won't help how awful they look during the day.

Recommended

L. dentata (Bigleaf Ligularia, Golden Groundsel) forms a clump of rounded, heart-shaped leaves. It grows 3–5' tall and spreads 3–4'. Clusters of orange-yellow flowers, held above the foliage, are borne in summer and early fall. '**Desdemona**' and '**Othello**' are two similar cultivars with orange flowers and purple-green foliage. They come fairly true to type when grown from seed.

L. przewalskii (Shevalski's Ligularia) also forms a clump but has deeply incised leaves. It grows 4–6' tall and spreads 2–4'. Yellow flowers are produced on long purple spikes in mid- and late summer.

L. stenocephala (Narrow-spiked Ligularia) has toothed rather than incised foliage and bears bright yellow flowers on dark purple-green

L. dentata (above), 'The Rocket' (below)

spikes. It grows 3–5' in height and width. The cultivar '**The Rocket**' has heart-shaped leaves with raggedly toothed margins. The leaf veins are dark, becoming purple at the leaf base.

Problems & Pests

Ligularias have no serious problems, though slugs can cause damage to the young foliage.

Lily-of-the-Nile

Agapanthus

Height: 18"–4' **Spread:** 12–24" **Flower color:** purple, blue, white
Blooms: mid-June through August **Hardiness:** hardy

LILY-OF-THE-NILE PLANTS MAKE WONDERFUL EVERGREEN BORDERS
and can provide winter greenery when combined with perennials that need
to be cut back in winter, such as sage. These plants also combine well with
Euryops Daisy and other winter-blooming perennials. The foliage can be
the focal point of a perennial garden, and the blooms are a bonus. One of the
drawbacks to the plant is that snails love to nest in its succulent foliage. Use
Sluggo™ snail bait to control this problem.

Planting

Seeding: Direct sow in spring; soil
temperature 55–59° F

Transplanting: Any time temperature above 28° F

Spacing: 12–24"

'Peter Pan' (above), Hybrid (below)

Growing

Lily-of-the-Niles prefer **full sun, partial shade** or **light, dappled shade**. Provide protection from the hottest afternoon sun. The soil should be **fertile, well drained** and preferably **moist**. Keep the plants well watered in the first year to help them get established; once well established, these plants are drought tolerant.

Dividing can be done at any time temperatures are 28° F or higher; however, the best time for dividing is just after the plants finish blooming. The plants need to be divided every three years to keep them at their blooming best. If left undivided for longer than three years, the plants will not produce as many flowers and will form a mound that makes division difficult.

Seedlings will be slow to develop and may not come true to type. You may, however, get some interesting variations. If you are growing these plants from seed and live in an area where the winter temperature consistently drops below 22° F, you must protect the seedlings over their first winter. If grown in pots, the plants will be easier to move to a protected location for the winter, and you can ensure the roots have good drainage. Lily-of-the-Nile plants should begin to flower after two to three years.

Tips

Lily-of-the-Nile plants are attractive whether they are in flower or not. The strap-like leaves are bright green and the round or pendulous

Agapanthus is derived from the Greek words agape, *meaning 'love,' and* anthos, *meaning 'flower.'*

clusters of flowers atop their long, straight stems make excellent companions to flowering shrubs. It is best to grow these plants in a south-facing bed because they tend to grow towards the sun.

These plants do not mind cool winters. They may freeze when temperatures get below 20° F but will recover shortly thereafter. To protect the plants over winter, provide a thorough mulch and plant them close to the foundation of the house. If grown in containers, they are easily placed into a sheltered location during frosty weather. They can also be lifted from the garden and stored for re-planting in spring.

Recommended

A. africanus (African Blue Lily) is an evergreen perennial growing 18–24" tall and spreading 12–18". Rounded clusters of deep blue flowers are borne in mid- to late summer. 'Albus' bears white flowers.

A. **Hybrids** are evergreen perennials that bloom in summer. There are many to choose from in various shades of blue and purple. 'Henryi' bears many pure white flowers above the 12"-tall foliage on stalks 18" tall.

The deep blue varieties of Lily-of-the-Nile look particularly striking with yellow-flowering plants such as Potentilla fruticosa.

'**Midnight Blue**' grows 3–4' tall and 24" wide and bears very deep blue flowers. '**Peter Pan**' produces a great number of blue flowers on flower stalks 18" tall. The foliage grows 12" tall and wide. '**Tinker Bell**' grows 24" tall and spreads 18". The foliage is variegated with white stripes and the flowers are light blue.

Problems & Pests

Slugs and snails may sometimes be problems. Bulb and root rot may occur in poorly drained soils.

A. africanus (this page)

Lion's Tail
Lion's Ear
Leonotis

Height: 4–6' or more **Spread:** 3–6' **Flower color:** orange, orange-red
Blooms: summer to fall **Hardiness:** semi-hardy

I WAS FIRST INTRODUCED TO THIS PLANT BY A CUSTOMER WHO
didn't know what it was. I didn't know what it was either, but I told her it
looked like a lion's tail. I looked it up under that name and, to my surprise,
there it was. Lion's Tail is a bold-looking
plant that looks dramatic in many landscapes. I like it as an accent
next to Mexican Sage.

Planting

Seeding: Direct sow in spring when soil temperature 55° F; indoors earlier

Transplanting: After last frost; from 4" pots or one-gallon containers

Spacing: 36"

Growing

Lion's Tail likes **full sun**, even in the hot Sacramento Valley. **Moderate to rich, well-drained** soil is preferred. This plant is very drought tolerant when established. Ensure you do not overwater when establishing. In spring cut the plant back by half and/or remove any winter-killed growth. Propagate by seed or by softwood cuttings in early summer.

Tips

Use Lion's Tail at the back of a border or as a specimen planting in a large container. It is a great choice for underneath the eaves on the south or west side of a house.

Recommended

L. leonurus is an erect, evergreen, shrubby perennial with aromatic foliage. The long, straight stems produce whorls of tubular, hairy flowers in shades of orange and orange-red.

Problems & Pests

This plant has infrequent problems with gray mold, whiteflies and spider mites.

The common name refers to the resemblance of the flowering stem to a lion's tail.

Lithodora

Lithodora

Height: 3–12" **Spread:** 1–4' **Flower color:** bright blue **Blooms:** late spring to summer **Hardiness:** semi-hardy

LITHODORA OFFERS THE MOST intensely blue blooms available on a low-growing perennial. The flowers stand out by themselves or combine wonderfully with Basket-of-Gold and other gray-foliage plants such as lavender cottons. It also mixes well with other low-growing perennials such as Candytuft and Phlox. Take cuttings occasionally and plant them into the center of the plant to hide the woody stems that can occur on older wood.

Planting

Seeding: Not recommended

Transplanting: Spring

Spacing: 12–36"

Growing

Lithodora prefers to grow in **full sun** in **well-drained, acidic, humus-rich** soil. Provide some afternoon shade in the hottest areas. Shear lightly after flowering to retain the shape of the plant and promote profuse flowering in the next season. Lithodora performs best and keeps it shape when fed once a month with organic fertilizers. Propagate by semi-hardwood cuttings in summer.

Tips

Lithodora is a good choice for rock gardens, as a groundcover for small areas or for edging at the top of retaining walls and around raised beds.

Recommended

L. diffusa (Lithospermum diffusum) is a prostrate, evergreen, shrubby perennial growing 6–12" tall and spreading 3–4'. Bright blue flowers are produced in clusters at the stem tips. '**Grace Ward**' grows 3" tall, spreads 12–24" and bears clear blue blooms. '**Heavenly Blue**' grows 6" tall and 24–30" wide. It has deep blue flowers.

Problems & Pests

Lithodora has infrequent problems with aphids or spider mites.

Lungwort

Pulmonaria

Height: 8–18" **Spread:** 12–24" **Flower color:** blue, red, pink, purple, white
Blooms: late winter to late spring **Hardiness:** hardy

LUNGWORTS ARE BEAUTIFUL EVERGREEN OR DECIDUOUS LOW-
growing perennials. The striking, sometimes variegated, foliage blends well
with other shade-loving perennials such as plantain lilies, ligularias, ferns
and columbines. Under trees and near water features, such a combination
creates a wonderful woodsy effect. Adding dwarf impatiens to such a mix
provides a splash of color during summer. The common name sounds rather
ugly; it does not reflect the beauty of these plants but refers
to a prior medicinal use.

Planting

Seeding: Start seed in containers outdoors in spring;
seedlings don't come consistently true to type

Transplanting: Spring or fall

Spacing: 12–24"

*Dry the spotted leaves and add them
to potpourri for visual interest.*

Growing

Lungworts prefer **partial shade to full shade**. The soil should be **fertile, humus rich, moist** and **well drained**. Rot can occur in very wet soil. Divide in late summer after flowering or in fall. Provide the newly planted divisions with lots of water to help them re-establish.

Shear plants back lightly after flowering to deadhead and keep plants tidy. The plants will immediately put out new foliage when sheared.

Tips

Lungworts are useful and attractive groundcover plants for shady borders, woodland gardens and pond and stream edges.

Recommended

P. angustifolia (Blue Lungwort) forms a mounded clump of foliage. The leaves have no spots. This species grows 8–12" tall, spreads 18–24" and bears clusters of bright blue flowers, held above the foliage, from late winter to early spring.

P. longifolia (Long-leaved Lungwort) forms a dense clump of long, narrow, white-spotted, green leaves. It grows 8–12" tall, spreads 12–24" and bears clusters of blue flowers in early to late spring, often before or as the foliage emerges.

P. saccharata (Bethlehem Sage) forms a compact clump of large, white-spotted, evergreen leaves. It grows 12–18" tall, with a spread of about 24". Purple, red or white flowers emerge in late winter to early spring. This species has given rise to many cultivars and hybrids.

P. saccharata cultivar (above), *P. saccharata* (below)

'Janet Fisk' is very heavily spotted and appears almost silvery. Its pink flowers mature to blue. '**Mrs. Moon**' has pink buds that open to a light purple-blue and leaves that are dappled with silvery white spots. '**Pink Dawn**' has dark pink flowers that age to purple.

Problems & Pests

These plants are generally problem free but may get powdery mildew if the soil dries out for extended periods. Remove and destroy damaged leaves.

Lupine

Lupinus

Height: 18–36" **Spread:** 12–24" **Flower color:** white, cream, yellow, pink, peach, red, blue, some bicolored **Blooms:** early to mid-summer
Hardiness: hardy

I USUALLY PLANT THESE WONDERFUL, COLORFUL PLANTS IN A bed by themselves. I border them with gray-foliage plants such as a *Santolina* specimen. I like to crowd them a little bit so that if they start to lean, they lean against each other. They make a great cutting flower and are deer and gopher resistant.

The fuzzy, peapod-like capsules that form on the spike once the flowers fade can be removed or left to ripen so the seeds can be collected.

Planting

Seeding: Soak seeds in warm water for 24 hours then direct sow in late fall to early spring; if you start seeds indoors you may need to place planted seeds in the refrigerator for four to six weeks after soaking and planting

Transplanting: Winter, spring

Spacing: 12–18"

Growing

Lupines grow best in **full sun** but tolerate light to partial shade. The soil should be of **average to high fertility, moist, light, well drained** and **slightly acidic.** Protect plants from drying winds.

Division is not required. Lupines dislike having their roots disturbed. Deadhead as the season progresses to encourage more flowering.

Tips

Lupines are wonderful when massed together in borders or in cottage and natural gardens.

These perennials can be rather short-lived. One solution is to leave just a couple of spikes in place once flowering is finished to allow some seedlings to fill in as the older plants die out. The self-seeded plants will not likely resemble the parents. You can also propagate by carefully removing the small offsets that develop at the base of the plants and re-planting them.

Recommended

There are many species of lupines, but they are rarely grown in favor

Russell Hybrids (this page)

of the many popular hybrids. Most lupines form a dense basal mound of foliage from which tall spikes emerge bearing many flowers.

Gallery Hybrids are dwarf hybrids, 18–24" tall and 12–18" wide. They are available with flowers in blue, red, pink, yellow or white.

New Generation Hybrids live longer, flower for a longer period and are more resistant to mildew than the older hybrids. The plants produce dense foliage and spikes of flowers in blue, red, pink, peach, yellow, cream and white on plants 36" tall and 18–24" wide. These plants usually do not require staking.

Russell Hybrids (above)

Russell Hybrids were among the first groups of hybrids developed. They grow about 24–36" tall and 12–18" wide and produce flowers in a wide range of solids and bicolors.

Problems & Pests

Lupines are susceptible to aphids and powdery mildew. Provide good air circulation to avoid mildew problems. Problems with slugs, snails, leaf spot, stem rot and damping off (in seedlings) can also occur, though infrequently.

Russell Hybrids (this page)

Lupines are in the same plant family as beans and peas. Do not eat lupine pods or seeds, however, as they cause stomach upset.

Mallow

Malva

Height: 8"–4' **Spread:** 12–24" **Flower color:** purple, pink, white, blue
Blooms: summer to fall **Hardiness:** hardy

THESE SHORT-LIVED PERENNIALS FLOWER abundantly, bringing life to any sunny spot in the garden that might otherwise look bland in summer. These plants make a great background for rose gardens or other perennial beds. In coastal regions of Northern California they will naturalize, needing little water in the summer. In the hotter interior valleys of the state they require regular watering.

Planting

Seeding: Direct sow in spring

Transplanting: Spring

Spacing: 12–24"

Mallows are reputed to have a calming effect when ingested and were used in the Middle Ages as antidotes for aphrodisiacs and love potions.

Growing

Mallows grow well in **full sun**. The soil should be of **average fertility, moist** and **well drained**. These plants are drought tolerant.

In very rich soils the plants may require staking. Cutting plants back by about half in late May will encourage more compact, bushy growth but will delay flowering by a couple of weeks. Deadhead the flowers to keep the plant blooming until October. Mallows do not need dividing.

Mallows are short-lived but self-seed readily. Transplant or thin out seedlings if they are too crowded.

'Primley Blue' (above), 'Zebrina' (below)

'Zebrina' (above), 'Primley Blue' (below)

Mallows can also be propagated by basal cuttings taken in spring.

Tips

Use mallows in a mixed border or in a wild or cottage garden. They make beautiful cut flowers. Regular light pruning to remove old flowers encourages new growth and more flowering.

Recommended

M. alcea (Hollyhock Mallow) is a loose, upright, branching plant. It grows 24"–4' tall, spreads 18–24" and bears pink flowers with notched petals all summer and into fall. **'Fastigiata'** is an upright plant growing to 36" tall and 12" wide. This cultivar resembles Hollyhock *(Alcea)* more than the species does.

M. moschata (Musk Mallow) is a bushy, upright plant with musk-scented leaves. It grows about 36"

tall, spreads about 24" and bears pale pink or white flowers all summer. **'Pirouette'** ('Alba') bears pure white flowers.

M. sylvestris (Cheeses) may be upright or spreading in habit. Plants of this species can grow 8"–4' tall and spread about 12–24". The pink flowers have darker veining and are produced all summer and often until the first frost. Many cultivars are available. **'Bibor Felho'** is an upright cultivar that has rosy purple flowers with darker purple veins. **'Primley Blue'** is a prostrate cultivar that grows only about 8" tall and has light purple-blue flowers. **'Zebrina'** has pale pink or white flowers with purple veins. This cultivar is an upright grower.

Problems & Pests

Problems with rust, leaf spot and spider mites can occur occasionally.

M. moschata (above), 'Fastigiata' (below)

Marsh Marigold
Cowslip
Caltha

Height: 9–24" **Spread:** 10–30" **Flower color:** yellow, white
Blooms: spring **Hardiness:** hardy

MARSH MARIGOLD IS PERFECT TO PLANT NEAR A DRIPPING FAUCET or under hydrangeas that are in a slightly wet area that doesn't drain well. On the coast, Marsh Marigold tolerates some shade in the afternoon. In the hotter valley areas it is best where it gets morning sun and afternoon shade. This plant is usually not available in nurseries, but specialty seed catalogs can fulfill your needs. And for the record, cows are not the only animal to slip because of the glossy green foliage…I have the grass stains to prove it.

Planting

Seeding: Direct sow in moist soil in late summer to early fall; seeds are unlikely to sprout before spring

Transplanting: Spring

Spacing: 10–30"

Growing

Marsh Marigold will grow in **full sun** or **partial shade**. The soil should be **constantly moist or wet**. This plant will even grow in water as deep as 6" but prefers shallower water. Divide in fall or spring every two or three years. A side dressing of organic fertilizer in mid-summer will encourage stronger growth during warmer weather.

Tips

Marsh Marigold is an ideal plant to include in a water, stream or bog garden. It grows and flowers quickly in spring then dies back after blooming. It is an excellent plant to use with plants that are slow to develop in spring but require more room later in summer.

Even if you aren't interested in having a water garden, you can still grow Marsh Marigold as long as you are willing to keep it very well watered. It works well in naturalized gardens; again, as long as there is adequate water.

Recommended

C. palustris grows to a height and spread of 18–24". Single yellow flowers bloom in spring. **Var.** *alba* has white flowers and is less vigorous than the species. It grows 9" tall and 12" wide. **'Flore Pleno'** has yellow double flowers. It grows 10" tall and wide. **Var.** *palustris* (Giant Marsh Marigold) is native to the Pacific Northwest and has bright yellow flowers. It is much larger than the other varieties, growing 24" tall and 28–30" wide.

Problems & Pests

Powdery mildew and rust can be problems. Well-watered, stress-free plants are less susceptible to these problems.

This plant was called Cowslip by dairy farmers because of the way it grows along streams, causing hoofed feet to slip on the banks.

Meadow Rue
Thalictrum

Height: 2–6' **Spread:** 12–24" **Flower color:** pink, purple, yellow, white
Blooms: spring, summer **Hardiness:** hardy

THEIR FOLIAGE ALONE MAKES MEADOW RUES A MUST FOR ALL
perennial gardens. The blooms are a bonus. Because the flower stalks grow
anywhere from two to six feet, these plants are usually relegated to the rear
of most perennial beds. I put them right out in the front of the bed and
combine them with spring-blooming perennials such as columbines. Other
semi-shade-loving plants add to the charm of an area planted with meadow
rues. These plants are available from the herb locations in most nurseries but
are not edible.

Planting

Seeding: Direct sow in fall or sow indoors in early spring; soil temperature at about 70° F

Transplanting: Spring

Spacing: 12–24"

Growing

Meadow rues prefer **light or partial shade** in **humus-rich, moist** and **well-drained** soil. Provide shelter from the wind. These plants rarely need to be divided. If necessary for propagation, divide in spring as the foliage begins to develop. They may take a while to re-establish once they have been divided or have otherwise had their roots disturbed.

'Lavender Mist' (above), 'Hewitt's Double' (below)

Tips

In the middle or at the back of a border, meadow rues make a soft backdrop for bolder plants and flowers. They are beautiful when naturalized in an open woodland or meadow garden.

These plants often do not emerge until quite late in spring. Mark the location where they are planted so that you do not inadvertently disturb the roots if you are cultivating the bed before they begin to grow. Combine these plants with evergreen plants to eliminate any bare spots in the garden left when the meadow rues go dormant in winter.

Do not position individual plants too close together because their stems can become tangled.

Recommended

T. aquilegifolium (Columbine Meadow Rue) forms an upright mound 24–36" tall and 12–18" wide. Pink or white plumes of flowers are borne in mid- to late spring. The leaves are similar in appearance to those of columbines (*Aquilegia* species). **'Thundercloud'** ('Purple Cloud') has dark purple flowers. **'White Cloud'** has white flowers.

T. delvayi (Yunnan Meadow Rue) forms a clump of narrow stems that usually need staking. It grows 3–4' tall or more, spreads 18–24" and bears fluffy purple or white flowers for an extended period from late spring to summer. **'Hewitt's Double'** is a popular cultivar that produces numerous tiny, purple, pompom-like flowers.

T. aquilegifolium (above), 'Hewitt's Double' (below)

T. rochebruneanum 'Lavender Mist' (Lavender Mist Meadow Rue) forms a narrow, upright clump 4–6' tall and 18–24" in spread. The summer blooms are lavender purple and have numerous distinctive yellow stamens.

Problems & Pests

Problems with powdery mildew, rust, smut and leaf spot can occur.

T. aquilegifolium (this page)

Meadowsweet

Filipendula

Height: 24"–8' **Spread:** 18–4' **Flower color:** white, pink **Blooms:** summer
Hardiness: hardy

THESE BOLD PLANTS MAKE GREAT ADDITIONS TO ANY CUTTING
bed. I like to use the cut flowers in arrangements with ferns. *F. vulgaris* is the
variety preferred in most Northern California gardens as it grows well in dry
conditions. *F. rubra* and *F. ulmaria* are great choices for gardens that don't
drain well or are bog-like in winter; these species mix well with other water-
loving plants.

Planting

Seeding: Sow seeds in containers in cold frame in fall. Keep soil evenly moist over winter to encourage even germination; seeds will germinate in spring.

Transplanting: Spring

Spacing: 18–36"

Growing

Grow *F. rubra* and *F. ulmaria* in **full sun** along the coast and in **partial to full shade** in the hot interior valleys, ensuring you keep the plants out of the afternoon sun. They like soil that is **deep, fertile, humus rich** and **moist.** Ensure you provide plenty of water; the soil can remain constantly moist. These two meadowsweets particularly like leaf compost mixed into the soil. Apply mulch to help keep the roots cool and moist.

F. vulgaris prefers to grow in **full sun** but benefits from afternoon shade in the hottest areas. Grow in a **dry, slightly alkaline** soil.

F. rubra (above), *F. ulmaria* (below)

Meadowsweet has been used for generations to treat such ailments as kidney stones. It contains salicylate, a precursor of everyday aspirin.

F. ulmaria (above), F. rubra (below)

Deadhead if you desire, but the faded seedheads are quite attractive when left in place.

Divide in spring or fall. You may need a sharp knife or old pruning saw to divide these plants because they develop thick, tough roots. *Filipendula* species tend to self-seed, so if dividing these perennials seems too daunting a task, you may find transplanting the seedlings an easier way to propagate.

Tips

All *Filipendula* species can be used effectively in natural or wild gardens. *F. rubra* and *F. ulmaria* are excellent for bog gardens or wet sites. Grow them alongside streams or in moist meadows. They are good choices for the back of a border, as long as they are kept well watered.

F. vulgaris is a good choice for dry areas in your garden.

Recommended

F. rubra (Queen-of-the-Prairie, Meadowsweet) forms a large, spreading clump 6–8' tall and 4' wide. It bears clusters of fragrant, pink flowers. 'Venusta' has deep pink to deep purple-pink flowers on red stems.

F. ulmaria (Meadowsweet, Queen of the Meadow) has large clusters of cream white flowers. It grows to be 24"–6' tall and 24–36" wide. In past times it was used to flavor mead and ale, and is now used to flavor vinegars and jams. It may also be made into a pleasant wine (much the same way as dandelion wine is made). 'Aurea' has yellow foliage that matures to light green as the summer progresses. '**Variegata**' has leaves that are striped or blotched with yellow.

F. vulgaris (Dropwort) is a low-growing species that prefers dry soil. It grows 24–36" tall and 18" wide. '**Flore Pleno**' ('Multiplex') has white double flowers. '**Rosea**' has pink flowers.

Problems & Pests
Powdery mildew, rust and leaf spot are rare problems.

In 16th-century England, herbs were strewn on floors to cushion the floor, freshen the air and combat infections. Filipendula was the herb Queen Elizabeth I preferred for this purpose.

F. *ulmaria* (above), F. *rubra* (below)

Monkey Flower
Mimulus

Height: 6–36" **Spread:** 12–36" **Flower color:** orange, yellow, burgundy, pink, red, cream **Blooms:** spring, summer **Hardiness:** hardy

SCARLET MONKEY FLOWER IS A NATIVE PLANT THAT MAKES A great addition to the garden. It is found in the wild along creeks and streams throughout the state and blooms from the middle of May through the middle of July. When the creeks dry up in summer, it goes dormant until the rains begin in fall. In the garden it should be well watered to extend the bloom period over the entire summer.

Planting
Seeding: Indoors in early spring

Transplanting: After last frost

Spacing: 10–12"

Growing

Monkey flower plants prefer **partial, light or full shade**. Protection from the afternoon sun will prolong the blooming of these plants. The soil should be **fertile, moist** and **humus rich**. Don't allow the soil to dry out. Propagate by seed or by division in spring. *M. luteus* self-seeds.

Tips

Monkey flower plants make an excellent addition to a bog garden or a border near a pond. In a flower-bed, border or container garden, these plants will need to be watered regularly. Most species become scraggly and unattractive in hot sun.

Recommended

M. cardinalis (Scarlet Monkey Flower) is an erect, branched perennial. It grows 24–36" tall and wide and produces scarlet flowers through summer. Yellow markings sometimes appear in the throat of the flowers. This species can be planted in full sun but is best in shade. It will bloom again if cut back after the first bloom cycle and fed lightly with liquid organic fertilizer.

M. x *hybridus* plants are upright with solid or spotted flowers. They grow 6–12" tall and spread 12". Seeds sown in spring provide summer blooms, and seedlings set out in spring will flower earlier. 'Calypso' bears a mixture of flower colors. 'Mystic' is compact and early flowering and offers a wide range of bright flowers in solids or bicolors. All are short-lived perennials, so take cuttings from your favorite colors and plant the cuttings through summer to ensure a steady supply of blooms. They benefit from having their roots mulched with leaf mold in mid-summer.

Alternate Species

M. luteus (Yellow Monkey Flower), not as common as *M.* x *hybridus*, is worth growing for its low, spreading habit and attractive yellow flowers. It grows about 12" tall and spreads up to 24". Yellow flowers, sometimes spotted with red or purple, bloom from late spring to summer.

Problems & Pests

Downy or powdery mildew, gray mold, whiteflies, spider mites and aphids can cause problems.

The genus name, Mimulus, *is from the Latin* mimos, *meaning 'to mimic,' referring to the flowers' resemblance to the face of a monkey.*

'Mystic'

Monkshood

Aconitum

Height: 3–5' **Spread:** 12"
Flower color: purple, blue, white
Blooms: mid- to late summer
Hardiness: hardy

MONKSHOODS ARE WONDERFUL BLUE-
flowering perennials, and their attractive foliage
makes them a great addition to any garden even
when they're not in bloom. On the coast they
grow very well in full sun but need a winter
chill to force the flowers. This can be accom-
plished by holding off on watering during the
plant's period of dormancy. Monkshoods combine well with coral bells and other perennials
that love shade and keep their foliage
through the winter.

*An older common name, Wolfsbane,
refers to the former use of these plants
as a wolf poison.*

Planting

Seeding: Germination may be irregular. Seeds sown directly in spring may bloom the following summer; seeds planted later will not likely bloom for another year.

Transplanting: Spring; bare-rooted tubers may be planted in fall. Some nurseries may carry these plants in bloom in June and July in one-gallon containers.

Spacing: 18"

Growing

Monkshoods prefer **light shade** but do very well along coastal California in full sun. They will grow in any **moist** soil but prefer a **rich** soil with lots of **organic matter** worked in. Monkshoods will do poorly when the weather gets hot, particularly if conditions do not cool down at night. Mulch the roots to keep them cool. These plants require a period of dormancy in winter. Plants die to the ground in winter, so mark the spot where they are planted. Taller selections may require staking, especially in windy areas.

Monkshoods prefer not to be divided because they may be a bit slow to re-establish. If division is desired to increase the number of plants, then it should be done in late fall or early spring. When dividing or transplanting monkshoods, the crown of each plant should never be planted lower than where it was previously growing. Burying the crown any deeper will cause it to rot and the plant to die.

'Bicolor' (above), *A.* x *bicolor* (below)

A. napellus (this page)

Tips

Monkshood plants are perfect for cool, boggy locations along streams or next to ponds. They make tall, elegant additions to a woodland garden in combination with lower-growing plants.

Do not plant monkshoods near tree roots because these plants cannot compete with trees.

All parts of monkshood plants are **poisonous**. Wash your hands if you have come in contact with the sap of the plants.

Recommended

A. x *bicolor* (Bicolor Monkshood) is a group of hybrids that contain several of the more popular cultivars. 'Bicolor' grows to 4' tall and bears blue and white flowers in late summer. The flower spikes are often branched. '**Bressingham Spire**' grows up to 36" tall and bears dark purple-blue flowers on strong spikes that need no staking.

A. napellus (Common Monkshood) is an erect plant that forms a basal mound of finely divided foliage. It grows 3–5' tall and bears dark purple-blue flowers from mid- to late summer.

Aconitum *comes from the Greek* akoniton, *meaning 'dart.' The ancient Chinese and Arabs used the juice of monkshood plants to poison arrow tips.*

Problems & Pests

Protect plants from slugs, snails and sow bugs while dormant. Remove mulch in fall to discourage these pests.

The upper petals of a monkshood flower are fused to make an enclosure that looks like the cowl worn by medieval monks.

Obedient Plant
False Dragonhead
Physostegia

Height: 12"–4' **Spread:** 24–36" **Flower color:** bright pink, purple-pink, blue-pink, white **Blooms:** mid-summer to early fall **Hardiness:** hardy

THIS HARDY PERENNIAL IS A must for Northern California gardeners who want a lot of cutting flowers. The term obedient comes from the flower's ability to bend in any direction the florists want it to. With its preference for full sun, this is an ideal plant for the hot interior valleys.

Planting

Seeding: Direct sow in early fall or spring; soil temperature 70–75° F. Protect fall-started seedlings from winter cold.

Transplanting: July; from 4" pots; later from one-gallon containers

Spacing: 24"

Growing

Obedient Plant prefers **full sun** and tolerates partial or light shade. The soil should be of **average fertility** and **moist**. Obedient Plant may become invasive in cool, moist soil. In a fertile soil this plant will be more vigorous and will possibly need staking. Choose a compact cultivar to avoid the need for staking. Divide in early to mid-spring, once ground can be worked, every two years to curtail invasiveness.

Cut the plants back by half in spring to prevent floppy summer flowers. Cut them to the ground after their bloom cycle and give a light feeding of liquid organic fertilizer.

Tips

Obedient Plant provides masses of colorful spikes in a border in late summer. It is also useful in a cottage, woodland or cut-flower garden.

Recommended

P. virginiana has a spreading root system from which upright stems sprout. It grows 24"–4' tall and spreads 24–36". The species bears blue-pink flowers. 'Alba' has pure white flowers and grows 18–24" tall. 'Variegata' has gray-green leaves with white margins and bright pink to blue-pink flowers. 'Vivid' is a dwarf, growing 12–24" tall. It produces bright purple-pink to rose pink flowers.

Problems & Pests

Slugs, snails and rust may cause occasional problems.

P. virginiana (above), 'Variegata' (below)

The flowers can be bent around on the stems and will stay put where you leave them. It is this unusual habit that gives rise to the name Obedient Plant.

Oriental Poppy
Papaver

Height: 18"–4' **Spread:** 18–36" **Flower color:** red, pink, white, purple
Blooms: spring and early summer **Hardiness:** hardy

I REMEMBER THE GARDEN OF MRS. DUGGAN NEXT DOOR TO MY grandparents' place in Willits. She had Oriental Poppy plants, and the large blooms looked as if they were created out of crepe paper by an expert in ikebana. The large seedpods look much like those of *Papaver somniferum* (Opium Poppy) but do not contain the narcotic. The tall Super Poppy Hybrids are now available for the warmer climates of Northern California.

Planting

Seeding: Sow seeds in containers in cold frame or direct sow in October

Transplanting: Early spring from six-packs; May through July from 4" pots

Spacing: 18–24"

Growing

Grow this plant in a location that receives **full sun**. The soil should be of **average fertility** and must be **well drained**. The plant will die back after flowering and send up fresh new growth in late summer. Division is rarely required but may be done in late summer to early fall once the new rosettes begin to form. Do not plant the Super Poppy Hybrids too deep; keep the crown of the plant at ground level.

The use of poppy seeds in cooking and baking can be traced as far back as the ancient Egyptians.

Tips

Small groups of Oriental Poppy look great in an early summer border.

Because it goes completely dormant by mid-summer, Oriental Poppy may leave a bare spot in a border. Plant it with plants that get bushy as summer wears on. Baby's breath and catmint plants make good companions and will fill in any blank spots left in the border later in summer.

When the foliage turns yellow after blooming, cut back Oriental Poppy to the ground or it will attract slugs.

If the stems of this plant are dwarfed, it is because the soil is too compact and infertile. Proper preparation of the bed with 50 percent compost will avoid this situation. Along coastal regions of Northern California, Oriental Poppy will need 0–10–10 fertilizer to encourage proper blooming.

Recommended

P. orientale forms an upright, oval clump 18"–4' tall and 24–36" in spread. It bears red, scarlet, pink or white flowers with prominent black stamens. **'Black and White'** has white flowers with black markings at the bases of the petals. **'Cedric Morris'** has large, soft pink flowers. **'Pizzicato'** is a dwarf cultivar, with flowers in a wide range of colors. It forms a mound 18–24" tall, with an equal spread. **Super Poppy Hybrids** were developed in California for our mild winters and summer heat. They grow 24–36" tall and wide and produce large flowers in shades of pink and purple. They bloom longer, grow faster, have longer stems and produce more vivid colors than other varieties.

Problems & Pests

Problems with powdery mildew, leaf smut, gray mold, root rot and damping off may occur. Oriental Poppy is deer resistant.

Peony

Paeonia

Height: 18"–4' **Spread:** 18"–4' **Flower color:** white, yellow, pink, red, purple
Blooms: spring, early summer **Hardiness:** hardy

PEONIES CAN BE FRUSTRATING TO GROW IN THE BAY AREA. THEY don't like heavy clay soil, they need perfect drainage, and they need a cold period to set the flowers. So why try to grow them when there are so many other wonderful plants that don't require special care? Because they are well worth the extra effort, and, like lilacs, they remind us of times past and our grandmothers' gardens.

Planting

Seeding: Not recommended; seeds may take two to three years to germinate and many more years to grow to flowering size

Transplanting: Spring from two-gallon containers; fall from tubers

Spacing: 24–36"

Growing

Peonies need at least **six hours of sun a day**. Provide afternoon shade from the hottest sun, especially inland. Peonies like **fertile, humus-rich, moist, well-drained** soil, to which lots of compost has been added. Prepare the planting area well in advance of planting. A good soil mix is one part peat moss, one part compost and one part planting mix or rich garden loam. Plant in a raised bed or make a mound of soil to provide the necessary drainage. A phosphorous fertilizer, such as bone meal or bulb food, may be mixed into the prepared soil before planting.

In the past, peonies were used to cure a variety of ailments. They are named after Paion, *the physician to the Greek gods.*

Division is not required, but it is usually the best way to propagate new plants and should be done in fall. Each division should have at least three buds or growth eyes, which are located on the top of the root mass.

Planting depth is very important for peonies. Tubers planted too deeply will not flower. The buds or growth eyes on the tuber should be 1" above the soil surface in mild winter areas for maximum exposure to winter conditions. Place wire tomato or peony cages around the plants in early spring to support the heavy flowers. The cage will be hidden by the foliage as it grows up into the wires.

Cut back the flowers after blooming and remove any blackened leaves. This will help to prevent the spread of gray mold. Cut stems to the ground in late fall. Red peonies are more susceptible to disease.

Tips

Peonies are wonderful plants that look great when combined with other early-flowering plants. They may be underplanted with bulbs and other plants that will die down by mid-summer, when the emerging foliage of peonies will hide the dying foliage of spring plants.

Plants purchased in containers can be planted easily and rarely experience any transplant shock. Purchased tubers should be full, succulent and free of bruises. They are available in catalogs but you might have better luck ordering them through your local nursery.

For the best performance, water regularly and fertilize twice a year, after flowering and in fall. Shelter the flowers from strong winds.

For cut flowers, take flowers when they are just beginning to open.

Make sure you leave some foliage on the stems you are cutting and never remove all the flowers in one season.

Recommended

Peonies may be listed as cultivars of a certain species or as hybrids. Hundreds are available. Check with your local garden center. In areas that don't get sufficiently cold, select peonies that are recommended for warmer areas.

P. lactiflora (Common Garden Peony, Chinese Peony) forms a clump of red-tinged stems and dark green foliage. It grows 2–4' tall and wide and bears fragrant, white or pink single flowers with yellow stamens in spring or early summer. It is the parent of many cultivars and hybrids. '**Festiva Maxima**' is a popular selection bearing fragrant white flowers with crimson specks at the base of the inner petals.

P. tenuifolia (Fernleaf Peony) grows 18–30" tall and wide and forms a clump of finely dissected, dark green foliage. Deep red flowers with yellow stamens bloom from mid- to late spring. '**Plena**' has double flowers.

Problems & Pests

Peonies may have trouble with *Verticillium* wilt, ringspot virus, tip blight, stem rot, gray mold, leaf blotch, nematodes or Japanese beetles.

Seed capsules forming (above)

P. lactiflora cultivar (center)

Peruvian Lily
Lily-of-the-Incas
Alstroemeria

Height: 2–5' **Spread:** 18–24" **Flower color:** red, orange, yellow, pink, salmon, coral, cream **Blooms:** late spring to mid-summer
Hardiness: hardy to semi-hardy

THE ORIGINAL *ALSTROEMERIA* PLANTS WERE DECIDUOUS AND had bright colors of orange, peach and salmon. The newer varieties are evergreen and tend to bloom in more pastel colors. All of these colorful additions to the garden can be used for spectacular bouquets. I planted a bed of these plants around some of the native oaks at my home. Because it is not wise to water oaks during the summer months, I let these plants dry out. With the winter rains, they reappeared to reward me with vase after vase of vibrant colors.

Planting

Seeding: Sow ripe seeds indoors in containers or direct sow in fall to early spring

Transplanting: Late winter to early spring

Spacing: 18"

Growing

Plant in **partial shade** to **full sun**. The soil should be **moist, acidic, well drained** and have **organic matter** added. Keep Peruvian Lily out of the hottest sun. Water a lot in summer, much less in winter. Feed once a month from late spring to early fall with a balanced fertilizer. It is a good idea to mulch for the first couple of years of growth, then mulch just in winter to protect the tubers from winter frost and freezing damage. This plant can be divided in spring or fall, but spring is preferable.

Plant tubers 8" deep in late summer or early fall. Handle the fragile tubers gently. It is best to leave the tubers to grow undisturbed once planted. They will self-sow.

Tips

Use Peruvian Lily under trees or on slopes. This plant blooms for a long time, making it ideal for a mixed border or cut-flower garden.

Contact with the foliage may cause skin irritation.

Recommended

A. **Litgu Hybrids** are derived from *A. litgu* and *A. haemantha*. They grow 2–5' in height and spread 18–24". The flowers have a range of colors including red, orange, yellow,

pink, salmon, coral, and cream. These hybrids come true from seed.

Problems & Pests

Slugs, snails, viral diseases and gray mold may present problems.

Phlox

Phlox

Height: 2"–4' **Spread:** 12–36" **Flower color:** white, red, purple, pink
Blooms: spring, summer **Hardiness:** hardy to semi-hardy

GARDEN PHLOX IS A GREAT CHOICE FOR THE CUTTING FLOWER BED. Phlox plants can withstand summer heat in the Central Valley although on very hot days the deep colors of the blooms may lighten, and you will need to mulch the plants to help them maintain their color. After blooming they need to be cut back to encourage more blooming. There are some mildew resistant varieties available such as 'David' and 'Bright Eyes.'

Planting

Seeding: Start seeds in containers in cold frame in fall or spring

Transplanting: Spring

Spacing: 12–36"

Growing

Garden Phlox and Wild Sweet William prefer to grow in **full sun** in **moist, fertile** soil. Provide shade from the hot afternoon sun to prevent the flower color from fading. Garden Phlox requires good air circulation to prevent mildew. Wild Sweet William is more resistant to powdery mildew. Pinch the tips off young plants to encourage bushy growth. Deadhead these species to extend the flowering season.

Divide in fall or spring. Mulch to keep the roots cool.

Grow Creeping Phlox in **partial shade** in **fertile, humus-rich, moist, well-drained** soil. Creeping Phlox spreads out horizontally as it grows—the stems grow roots where they touch the ground. Propagate by detaching and re-planting the rooted stems in spring or early fall. Do not prune Creeping Phlox in fall; it is an evergreen and will have next spring's flowers already forming.

Moss Phlox prefers to grow in **full sun** to **light shade** in **well-drained, moderately fertile** soil. Keep Moss Phlox in light shade if your area is on the dry side. Cut the plant back by half when flowering is finished.

Tips

Low-growing species are useful in a rock garden or at the front of a

P. paniculata (above), *P. subulata* (below)

P. paniculata (above & bottom)

P. maculata (center)

border. They need to be divided occasionally to increase vigor and extend bloom time. Taller species may be used in the middle of a border, where they are particularly effective if planted in groups.

Recommended

P. maculata (Wild Sweet William, Early Phlox) forms an upright clump of hairy stems and narrow leaves that are sometimes spotted with red. It grows 24–36" tall and spreads 18–24". Pink, purple or white flowers are borne in conical clusters in the first half of summer. This species has good resistance to powdery mildew. **'Omega'** bears white flowers with light pink centers. **'Rosalinde'** bears dark pink flowers.

P. paniculata (Garden Phlox) blooms in summer. This species has many cultivars that vary greatly in size, growing 20"–4' tall and spreading 24–36". Many colors are available, often with contrasting centers. **'Bright Eyes'** bears light pink flowers with deeper pink centers. **'David'** bears white flowers and is resistant to powdery mildew. **'Starfire'** bears crimson-red flowers.

P. stolonifera (Creeping Phlox) is a low, spreading plant that grows 4–6" tall, spreads about 12" and bears flowers in various shades of purple in spring. This species tolerates heavy shade and was named Perennial Plant of the Year in 1990 by the Perennial Plant Association.

P. subulata (Moss Phlox, Moss Pinks) is a very low-growing plant, only 2–6" tall, with a spread of 20".

The species and its cultivars bloom in flushes from April to August. **'Candy Stripe'** bears bicolored pink and white flowers. This cultivar often blooms again in fall.

Problems & Pests

Phloxes can have problems with powdery mildew and red spider mites. They may also be afflicted with stem canker, rust, leaf spot, leaf miners and caterpillars.

Phlox comes in many forms from low-growing creepers to tall, clump-forming uprights. The many species can be found in varied climates from dry, exposed mountainsides to moist, sheltered woodlands.

P. paniculata (above), P. subulata (below)

Pincushion Flower

Scabiosa

Height: 12–30" **Spread:** 12–24" **Flower color:** white, lavender, blue, pink
Blooms: end of May to frost **Hardiness:** hardy

PINCUSHION FLOWERS ARE GREAT FOR THE CUTTING GARDEN.
The cut flowers last for at least two weeks, and the seedpods can be added to
dried arrangements. The blue flowers can add a cool touch to otherwise hot-
looking areas of the garden. I had a plant in a 6" container for several years
without transplanting. It seems it did not mind being root-bound.

Planting

Seeding: Direct sow in spring
or summer or start freshly
ripened seeds in containers in
cold frame in fall or early
spring

Transplanting: Mid-March
through June; from 4" pots

Spacing: 24"

Growing

Pincushion flower plants prefer **full sun** but tolerate partial shade. Keep them out of the hottest afternoon sun. The soil should be **light, moderately fertile, neutral** or **alkaline** and **well drained**. Ensure you provide adequate water, but unless they've dried out completely, pincushion flowers will recover rapidly if they have been forgotten on your regular watering schedule.

When transplanting from 4" pots, loosen the roots. Divide in early spring whenever the clumps become overgrown.

The plant will respond well to monthly feedings with liquid organic fertilizer, and applying a liquid 0–10–10 fertilizer will force the plant to bloom more often.

Tips

These plants look best when they are planted in groups in a bed or border.

Remove the flowers as they fade to promote a longer flowering period. Cutting flowers at their peak every few days for indoor floral arrangements will make this maintenance chore more enjoyable.

Recommended

S. caucasica is a clump-forming plant that grows 18–30" tall and 12–24" wide and bears lavender or pale blue flowers. '**Blue Perfection**' produces lavender to blue flowers. '**Fama**' has sky blue flowers with silvery white centers on branching stems. **House's Hybrids** (Isaac House Hybrids) bear large, unkempt-looking blue flowers. '**Miss Wilmont**' has white flowers.

Several hybrids have been developed from crosses between *S. caucasica* and *S. columbaria*, a smaller species. These hybrids may be listed as cultivars of either species. '**Butterfly Blue**' grows to 24" and bears lavender blue flowers. '**Pink Mist**' grows 12–16" tall and wide, bearing many pink blooms.

Problems & Pests

Aside from occasional encounters with aphids, pincushion flower plants rarely present problems.

The genus name, Scabiosa, *refers to the traditional use of this plant to treat scabies.*

Plantain Lily
Hosta
Hosta

Height: 4–36" **Spread:** 12–36" **Flower color:** white, purple
Blooms: summer and fall **Hardiness:** hardy

ALTHOUGH I HAVE KNOWN ABOUT AND ADMIRED PLANTAIN LILY plants all my life, I was denied the pleasure of growing them because they are often beset with slugs and snails. For many years the only effective slug bait available was Metaldehyde, and I refused to use it because it can be deadly to wildlife and pets. Now there are slug baits on the market that are perfectly safe around all wildlife and pets. The new baits contain iron phosphate, which breaks down into an organic fertilizer. Slugs and snails that take the bait crawl out of view before expiring.

Plantain lilies are considered by some gardeners to be the ultimate shade plants. They are available in a wide variety of leaf shapes, colors and textures.

Planting

Seeding: Direct sow in garden or in cold frame in spring; young plants can take three or more years to reach flowering size

Transplanting: Spring

Spacing: 12–36"

Growing

Plantain lilies prefer **light shade, partial shade** or **full shade.** Some species tolerate full sun in cooler areas. Morning sun is preferable to afternoon sun. The soil should be **fertile, moist** and **well drained,** but most soils are tolerated. Plantain lilies are fairly drought tolerant, especially if mulched to help retain soil moisture.

Division is not required, but it can be done every few years in spring or summer to propagate attractive cultivars. Small offshoot plants around the main plant can be transplanted.

Tips

Plantain lilies make wonderful woodland plants, especially when combined with ferns and other fine-textured plants. Plantain lilies are also useful in a mixed border, especially to hide the ugly, leggy lower stems and branches of some shrubs. The dense growth and thick shade-providing leaves of these plants make them excellent choices for suppressing weeds. When purchasing plantain lilies, check what sunlight exposure the plants can tolerate.

The flowers of plantain lilies are attractive and often fragrant. However, the flower colors often clash with the leaves, which are the main decorative feature of the plant. If you don't like the look of the flowers, feel free to remove them before they open. It won't hurt the plants.

Some gardeners feel that the foliage of plantain lilies does not develop its best coloring and shape unless the plants are left undivided for many years. It is easy to detach small segments from the edge of the plant's clump to propagate new plants without digging up the entire plant and disturbing the roots.

Recommended

Plantain lilies have been subjected to a great deal of breeding and hybridizing, resulting in hundreds of cultivars, many whose exact parentage is uncertain. For the sake of simplicity, the following cultivars have been grouped with the most generally accepted parent species, but you may find them listed under other names.

H. fortunei (Fortune's Hosta) has broad, dark green foliage and bears lavender flowers in mid-summer. It quickly forms a dense clump of foliage 12–24" tall and 24–36" wide. 'Albomarginata' has cream or white margins on the leaves. 'Aureo-marginata' has irregular yellow margins on the leaves; it tolerates sun better than many cultivars. 'Francee' has puckered, dark green leaves with narrow, white margins.

H. plantaginea (Fragrant Hosta) has glossy, bright green leaves with distinctive veins. It grows 18–30" tall, spreads to about 36" and bears large, white, fragrant flowers in late summer. 'Aphrodite' has white double flowers. 'Honeybells' has sweetly fragrant, light purple flowers. 'Royal Standard' is a low-growing cultivar 4–8" tall and up to 36" wide with deeply veined dark green leaves and light purple flowers. 'Venus' is slightly smaller than the species and produces white double flowers.

H. ventricosa (Blue Plantain Lily) forms clumps 20–24" tall and 36" wide. The leaves are dark green, glossy, heavily veined and heart-shaped. In late summer, it bears violet blue to deep purple flowers on 36" stems. 'Aureo-maculata' has yellow-green foliage with green margins. 'Aureo-marginata' has green leaves with yellow to creamy white, irregular margins.

Problems & Pests

Slugs, snails, leaf spot, crown rot and chewing insects such as black vine weevils are all possible problems for plantain lilies.

Purple Coneflower

Echinacea

Height: 18"–4' **Spread:** 18–24" **Flower color:** purple, white; rusty-orange centers **Blooms:** late spring to summer **Hardiness:** hardy

I USED TO THINK OF THE PRAIRIES AS SEMI-DESERT AREAS THAT John Wayne drove a wagon over, dust billowing behind him. When I first saw the prairies in Minnesota, I realized that the prairies are often very moist and very beautiful. There I saw Joe Pye Weed, Purple Coneflower and grasses all mixed up in an area that would have been impassable if not for the animal trails. Purple Coneflower lends itself to any informal mix of perennials. Despite its origins in wet regions of North America, it is adaptable to almost any garden situation.

Planting

Seeding: Direct sow in spring

Transplanting: Spring on the coast; fall in the hot interior valleys

Spacing: 18"

Growing

Purple Coneflower grows well in **full sun** or very **light shade**. Any well-drained soil is tolerated, but an **average or rich soil** is preferred. This plant prefers regular watering, but its thick taproot makes it drought resistant. However, in the interior valleys it will require additional water. Pinch plants back in early summer to encourage bushy growth that is less prone to mildew. Divide every four years in spring or fall.

Deadheading early in the season is recommended to prolong the flowering season. Later in the season you may wish to leave the flowerheads in place to go to seed. Purple Coneflower is the favorite food of migrating finches.

E. purpurea (above)

Echinacea was an important medicinal plant for many Native Americans. Today it remains a popular immunity booster in herbal medicine. The root is usually harvested when the plant is at least two to three years old.

Planting (below) of 'Magnus' (left) and 'White Swan' (right)

Tips

Use Purple Coneflower in meadow gardens, open woodlands, informal borders and mass plantings or as individual plants. This plant performs well in the heat and can be used effectively next to south-facing walls.

Purple Coneflower may self-seed. If you don't want more plants, remove all the flowerheads as they fade.

Recommended

E. purpurea is an upright plant covered with prickly hairs. It grows 24"–4' tall and spreads 18–24". Cultivars are generally about half the height of the species. Purple flowers with orangy centers may begin appearing in late spring, and the plant continues to bloom until the first frost. **'Magnus'** bears large, purple, orange-centered flowers

E. purpurea (above), 'Magnus' (below)

up to 7" across. **'White Lustre'** bears white flowers with orange centers, and it grows 24–36" tall. **'White Swan'** is a compact plant 18–24" tall with white flowers.

Problems & Pests

Powdery mildew is the biggest problem for Purple Coneflower. Vine weevils may attack the roots, and leaf miners, bacterial spot and gray mold may also be troublesome.

Purple Coneflower yields good cut flowers. The dry flowerheads may be left on the plants and make an interesting feature in fall and winter gardens.

'White Lustre' (this page)

Rock Cress
Wall Rock Cress
Arabis

Height: 4–8" **Spread**: 8–18" **Flower color:** white, pink, purple
Blooms: spring **Hardiness:** hardy to semi-hardy

ROCK CRESS PLANTS MAKE A BEAUTIFUL GROUNDCOVER WITH
Paper Whites *(Narcissus papyraceus)*. This combination creates a permanent
planting with loads of spring color. Most of the soils in California are lime-
based, alkaline soils, which are ideal for *Arabis* plants.

Planting

Seeding: Start in containers in early spring; keep in full sunlight until they
germinate

Transplanting: May through July; from 4" pots and one-gallon containers

Spacing: 8–12"

Growing

Rock cress plants prefer **full sun**. The soil should be **average** or **poor, well drained** and **alkaline**. These plants will do best in a climate without extremely hot summers. Keep *A. blepharophylla* out of the hot afternoon sun and ensure it has adequate moisture.

Cutting the plants back after flowering will keep them neat and compact. Divide in early fall every two or three years. Stem cuttings are usually the best way to propagate new plants; they can be taken from the new growth and started in summer.

Tips

Rock cress species make a great addition to rock gardens, rock walls or border edging. They are also useful as groundcovers on exposed slopes or as companion plants in a natural setting with small bulbs.

A. caucasica can be an aggressive grower and should not be planted where it may overwhelm slower-growing plants. *A. blepharophylla* should not be planted with aggressive, spreading plants because it will likely be overrun.

Recommended

A. blepharophylla (California Rock Cress) grows 4–8" tall and 8–12" wide. The fragrant, pink to purple flowers are borne in clusters in early to mid-spring.

A. caucasica (Wall Rock Cress) grows 6–8" tall and spreads 12–18". In late spring it bears fragrant white flowers. **'Flore Pleno'** ('Plena') has pure white double flowers.

A. caucasica (this page)

Arabis *resembles* Aubrieta, *and both are commonly known as rock cress. Make sure you know the scientific name of the plant you want before going to the garden center to buy it.*

'Variegata' (*A. ferdinandi-coburgii* 'Variegata') has cream- or sometimes pink-tinged foliage and is a low-maintenance plant.

Problems & Pests

White rust, rust and downy mildew are the most common problems. Aphids are occasionally troublesome, along with *Arabis* midge, which causes deformed shoots that should be removed and destroyed.

Russian Sage

Perovskia

Height: 30"–4' **Spread:** 36" **Flower color:** blue
Blooms: late spring to summer **Hardiness:** hardy

RUSSIAN SAGE PLANTS ARE MY FAVORITES FOR difficult areas in the interior valleys of California. These plants tolerate heat and are quite drought tolerant once established. Because these plants go dormant in winter, plant them among evergreen plants or in an area that is not a focal point of your landscape. The blooms of these sages add a wispy tone to any floral bouquet, and winter-blooming annuals such as Pot Marigold, Iceland Poppy, pansies or primroses combine well with Russian sages. *Perovskia atriplicifolia* was the 1995 Perennial Plant of the Year as selected by the Perennial Plant Association.

Planting

Seeding: Not recommended; germination can be erratic

Transplanting: Spring

Spacing: 36"

The airy habit of these plants creates a mist of silver-purple in the garden.

Growing

Russian Sage plants prefer **full sun**. The soil should be **poor to moderately fertile** and **well drained**.

Russian Sage plants do not need dividing. The plants send out colonies, which can be harvested from the mother plant in the fall. To keep the new growth fresh and vigorous, gently pull off the old stalks when the plant goes completely dormant and dies to the ground. Regular deadheading will lengthen the bloom period.

I find the best way to propagate Russian sage plants is to take root cuttings in January and transplant them to the garden when the new shoots appear. Softwood cuttings taken in late spring are another method of propagating.

Tips

The silvery foliage and blue flowers of Russian sages combine well with other plants in the back of a mixed border and can soften the boldness of daylilies. These are great plants for a hot, dry spot in the garden, in a natural garden or on a dry bank.

Recommended

P. atriplicifolia is a long-lived, erect plant 3–4' tall. It has silver-gray foliage and small lavender blue flowers. 'Filagran' has delicate foliage and an upright habit and is slightly shorter than the species, growing 30–36" tall. 'Longin' is narrow and erect and has more smoothly edged leaves than other cultivars.

The flowers of Russian sage look great in both fresh bouquets and dried arrangements.

P. 'Blue Spire' is an upright plant with deep blue flowers and feathery leaves.

Problems & Pests

Russian sages rarely suffer pest problems, but the plants may rot in wet winters.

Salvia
Sage
Salvia

Height: 1–10' **Spread:** 18"–5' **Flower color:** blue, red, purple, pink, white; bracts in pink, purple, maroon **Blooms:** spring, summer, fall **Hardiness:** hardy to semi-hardy

IN THE LAST 10 YEARS, NORTHERN CALIFORNIANS HAVE BEEN fortunate to introduce to their gardens over 55 varieties of salvias. Many varieties attract hummingbirds and butterflies and are resistant to deer, rabbits and other wildlife. We have mentioned a few salvias in these pages, but it's hoped that we'll whet your appetite to learn and plant more. Most have fragrant foliage and some can be added to tea or as a seasoning to meat and fish dishes.

Planting

Seeding: Indoors in mid-winter; direct sow in spring

Transplanting: After last frost

Spacing: Slightly less than the plant spread

Growing

All salvias prefer **full sun** but tolerate partial to light shade. The soil should be **moist** and **well drained** and of **average to rich fertility,** with lots of **organic matter**. To keep plants producing flowers, ensure they receive adequate water and deadhead regularly.

Propagate by seed, by basal or softwood cuttings in spring or by semi-hardwood cuttings in summer. *S. officinalis* can be layered easily as the branches send down roots where they touch the ground.

Tips

The following salvias are useful planted in groups in beds and borders. They also make excellent container plants.

Recommended

S. clevelandii (California Blue Sage, Cleveland Sage) is an evergreen shrub with arching stems and a rounded habit growing 3–5' tall and 5–8' wide. It has aromatic gray-green leaves that are especially fragrant after a rainstorm. Fragrant flowers in shades of lavender, violet and blue bloom from mid-April through the end of June. This species is drought tolerant. The foliage makes a wonderful fragrant tea.

S. elegans (right)

S. mexicana cultivar (above), 'Bethellii' (below)

Remove spent blooms to encourage further blooming. It will naturalize after the first year and is effective under native oak trees in the hot afternoon sun.

S. elegans (Pineapple Sage) is an erect perennial reaching 6' in height and spreading 3–4'. In frost-free areas it produces clusters of bright scarlet flowers from late fall to spring. Frost stops the plant from blooming. The bright green leaves emit a mild pineapple aroma. **'Scarlet Pineapple'** bears more flowers and has a stronger aroma than the species. It grows 3–4' tall and wide. The fresh leaves of both selections are used in cool drinks, teas and fruit salads. The flowers add flavor and color to desserts and salads.

S. involucrata (Rosy-leaf Sage) is a fast-growing, shrubby perennial reaching a height of 5–6' and a spread of 3–5'. Dense, spiky clusters of purplish red flowers are produced from mid-summer to mid-fall. Each flower is surrounded by pink to purplish pink bracts that fall away as the flower opens. This sage will suffer if the temperature falls below 25° F. It will perform best when given afternoon shade. **'Bethellii'** bears flowers in shorter, rounded clusters.

S. leucantha (Mexican Bush Sage) is a shrubby perennial growing 3–4' tall and 4–6' wide. White flowers with purple calyxes are produced freely from late spring to late fall. This species needs to be cut to the base in winter to allow new spring growth. **'Midnight'** ('Purple Velvet') bears purple flowers and purple calyxes.

S. mexicana (Mexican Sage) is a large, erect, shrubby perennial reaching a height of 10–12' and a width of 3–5'. It produces aromatic, pine-scented foliage and spikes of blue, purple or violet flowers from early fall to spring in frost-free areas. Frost will stop this plant from flowering. Provide adequate water; overwatering will result in brittle stems. The stems can be cut back after the flowers fade to keep the plant compact. Shelter from strong winds.

S. officinalis (Purple Sage, Garden Sage, Common Sage) is the well-known culinary and medicinal sage. It is a shrubby, short-lived perennial 30–36" tall and wide, with aromatic gray-green leaves that have white, downy undersides. Clusters of violet blue, sometimes pink or white, flowers are produced from late spring to summer. Cut the plants back to just above the new growth when the new growth first appears. Plants will need replacing when they start looking scraggly or leggy. **'Tricolor'** has white or cream variegation on the leaf margins and the new leaves are flushed with purple-pink. It bears lavender blue flowers.

Problems & Pests

Salvias experience occasional problems with aphids and a few fungal diseases. Seedlings are prone to damping off. Plants can suffer from poor drainage and too much water.

S. officinalis cultivar (bottom right)

Cut flowers of salvias last a long time in floral arrangements. As dried flowers they combine well in arrangements with eucalyptus.

Sandwort

Arenaria

Height: 2–4" **Spread:** 12–24" **Flower color:** white with yellow centers
Blooms: late spring to early summer **Hardiness:** hardy

SANDWORTS ARE OFTEN USED AS GROUNDCOVERS BUT ARE BEST used in dry-laid rock walls. The evergreen moss-like foliage is covered with white flowers in late spring and early summer. These plants can spread into the garden. They are easy to pull out and transplant to other locations in the garden if more plants are desired.

Planting

Seeding: Direct sow mid-February; indoors in flats in fall

Transplanting: Mid-February to mid-March

Spacing: 10"

Growing

Sandworts like to grow in **full sun** or **light shade**. The soil should be of **average fertility, moist, sandy** and **well drained**. The plants tolerate the heat of the interior valley, though with a shortened bloom cycle. Divide in spring or fall, whenever the center of the plant begins to thin out. Plants will self-seed in good garden conditions and may become invasive.

Tips

Sandworts do well in a rock garden, on a stone wall or between the paving stones of a path.

These plants like to be watered regularly but don't like standing water. Plant sandworts beneath taller shrubs and apply a fine-textured mulch to the soil surface. Both the mulch and the sandwort plants themselves will protect the roots of the larger shrubs. Sandworts have shallow roots and will not compete with the larger shrubs.

Recommended

A. montana (Mountain Sandwort) has trailing stems that reach up to 4" in height and spread 12–24". Growing in full sun will give the best results.

A. verna (Moss Sandwort) has evergreen, moss-like foliage on plants 2–4" tall. It works well between stepping stones. **Var.** *caespitosa* (*Sagina subulata*) (Irish Moss) is 2" tall and bears star-shaped, white flowers. One problem of Irish Moss is its tendency to mound up. This can be controlled by cutting out the center of each mound and rolling the plant with a lawn roller.

Problems & Pests

Sandworts can suffer occasional problems with slugs, snails, cutworms, rust and smut.

A. montana (above), *A. verna* var. *caespitosa* (below)

Sea Holly
Eryngium

Height: 12"–4' **Spread:** 18–24" **Flower color:** purple, blue, white
Blooms: summer, sometimes to early fall **Hardiness:** hardy

SEA HOLLY PLANTS MAKE AN INTERESTING BORDER AROUND
other perennial beds that require little, if any, summertime watering. They
combine well with most sages and yarrows. For dried flower arrangements,
the flowerheads can be placed on the flowerless stems of other plants for an
interesting display.

*Several centuries ago in England, the roots
of one* Eryngium *species were candied and
used as an aphrodisiac lozenge.*

Planting

Seeding: Direct sow freshly ripened seed in fall

Transplanting: Spring

Spacing: 12–24"

Growing

Grow sea hollies in **full sun**. The soil should be of **poor to average fertility** and **well drained**. The long taproot makes these plants fairly drought tolerant but averse to prolonged periods without water. Good drainage is essential as sea hollies do not like to be wet in winter.

These plants are very slow to re-establish after dividing. Root cuttings should be taken in late winter.

Tips

The long-lasting flowers of sea hollies look attractive with other flowers in a border and are distinctive when used in fresh or dried arrangements. These plants have short stems. The flowerheads must be removed and attached to long florists' wire before adding them to an arrangement. Sea hollies are also interesting in naturalized gardens.

Recommended

E. alpinum (Alpine Sea Holly) grows 24–48" tall. This species has soft, spiny bracts and steel blue or white flowers. Several cultivars are available in different shades of blue.

E. amethystinum (Amethyst Sea Holly) grows 18–30" tall and 18–24" wide. It produces steel blue to amethyst purple flowers.

E. alpinum

E. varifolium (Moroccan Sea Holly) grows 12–16" tall. It has dark green leaves with silvery veins and gray-purple flowers with blue bracts.

Problems & Pests

The roots of sea hollies may rot if the plants are left in standing water for long periods. Slugs, snails and powdery mildew may be problems.

Sea Pink
Thrift
Armeria

Height: 6–18" **Spread:** 8–12" **Flower color:** red, pink, white
Blooms: late spring to early summer **Hardiness:** hardy

SEA PINKS CAN BE COMBINED WITH OTHER low-growing perennials to form patterns of different textures. Irish Moss and Scotch Moss would work well with a sea pink specimen for this purpose. Sea pinks are ideal plants to place around trees in lawns. They look great and prevent the need to mow right up to the tree, thereby protecting the tree trunks from the lawnmower. The common name refers to the plants' ability to tolerate coastal conditions.

Attract bees and butterflies to a seaside garden with clumps of dependable sea pinks.

Planting

Seeding: Start seeds in spring or fall; soak for a few hours before planting

Transplanting: Spring; from six-packs

Spacing: 10"

Growing

Sea pinks require **full sun**. The soil should be **poor** or **moderate** and **well drained**. Sea pinks are very drought tolerant. Shearing after a bloom cycle will prolong the already lengthy bloom cycle into the fall. Divide in spring or fall when you want more plants or when the center of a plant dies out; division at least every three to four years will keep the plants looking their best.

Tips

Sea pinks are great for seaside gardens because they tolerate salt spray. Use these little gems in rock gardens or at the front of a border.

If your plant seems to be dying out in the middle of the clump, try cutting it back hard. New shoots should fill in quickly.

Recommended

A. 'Bee's Ruby' produces bright pink flowers on 12–18" stems. It spreads 8–12" wide.

A. maritima is the most used and most variable Sea Pink. The flowering stems rise to 6–12" and bear white to deep pink flowers. 'Alba' has white flowers. 'Bloodstone' has dark red flowers. 'Rubrifolia' has rose-pink flowers and purple-red leaves.

Problems & Pests

Problems are rare with these durable plants. They may occasionally suffer from rust or attacks by aphids.

A. maritima (above & bottom)

'Alba' (center)

Shasta Daisy
Leucanthemum

Height: 24"–4' **Spread:** 24" **Flower color:** white; yellow centers
Blooms: early summer to fall **Hardiness:** hardy

SHASTA DAISY IS A WONDERFUL ADDITION TO YOUR PERENNIAL border. Since its introduction, Shasta Daisy has been the parent of several varieties of white daisy. All of these daisies are long-lasting cut flowers. Shasta Daisy was introduced by the famous plant breeder Luther Burbank (1849–1926), who also introduced the Burbank potato. One of my favorite photographs shows Luther Burbank, Henry Ford and Thomas A. Edison sitting on the front porch of the Burbank home and seed-testing ground in Santa Rosa, California.

Planting

Seeding: Direct sow or start seeds indoors in spring; soil temperature 70–75° F

Transplanting: Spring

Spacing: 24"

Growing

Shasta Daisy prefers **full sun** but will appreciate afternoon shade in hot areas. The soil should be **fertile, moist** and **well drained**. Pinch or trim plants back in spring to encourage compact, bushy growth. Divide every two years in spring to maintain the plants' vigor.

Tips

Use Shasta Daisy in a border where it can be grown as a single plant or massed in groups. Drifts of Shasta Daisy are effective combined with such perennials as Purple Coneflower, Butterfly Weed or coreopsis plants. These plants all bloom at different times during the season and attract a variety of butterflies.

Recommended

L. x *superbum* forms a large clump of dark green leaves. The species bears white, yellow-centered flowers all summer, often until the first frost. 'Alaska' bears large flowers and is hardier than the species. 'Esther Reed' is slightly smaller than the species and bears white double flowers for an extended period. 'Marconi' has large semi-double or double flowers.

Problems & Pests

Watch for slugs and snails. Shasta Daisy may have occasional problems with aphids, leaf spot, leaf miners and root crown gall.

To produce the original Shasta Daisy, Luther Burbank worked with several species of daisies near Mount Shasta, California.

Soapwort

Saponaria

Height: 6–24" **Spread:** 18–36" **Flower color:** pink, white, red
Blooms: spring, summer **Hardiness:** hardy

SOAPWART PLANTS ARE TOUGH AND CAN OFTEN BE FOUND ALONG
deserted railway right-of-ways. They are best used between stepping stones
or cracks in walls as they can handle light foot traffic. They bloom from mid-
spring to early summer, and regular summer watering will keep the plant
looking good all year long. The common name of these plants refers to the
sudsy, detergent-like lather created when its roots are crushed in water.

Saponin-rich plants such as S. officinalis *were once used as soap.
The roots create suds when mixed with water.*

Planting

Seeding: Start seeds in early spring. Keep the planted seeds in a cool, dark place, about 60–65° F, until they germinate; then move into a lighted room.

Transplanting: Spring

Spacing: 18"

Growing

Soapworts grow best in **full sun**. The soil should be of **average fertility, neutral to alkaline, moist** and **well drained**. Poor soils are tolerated. Divide in spring every few years to maintain vigor and control spread. The plants are self-grooming.

Tips

Use soapworts in borders, in rock gardens and on rock walls. Soapworts can overwhelm less vigorous plants. *S. ocymoides* should be cut back after flowering to keep the plant neat, compact and attractive.

Recommended

S. ocymoides (Rock Soapwort) forms a low, spreading mound. It grows

S. officinalis (above), 'Rosea Plena' (below)

6–12" tall and spreads 24–36". The plant is completely covered in bright pink flowers in late spring and continues to flower sporadically all summer. **'Alba'** has white flowers. **'Rubra Compacta'** is very low growing, with dark pink flowers.

S. officinalis (Soapwort, Bouncing Bet) is an upright plant up to 24" tall and about 18" in spread. This plant is aggressive and can quickly spread farther with good growing conditions. It bears pink, white or red flowers from summer to fall. **'Rosea Plena'** bears fragrant, pink double flowers in early summer. Cultivars are not as invasive as the species.

Stokes' Aster

Stokesia

Height: 12–24" **Spread:** 18" **Flower color:** blue, purple-blue, white
Blooms: summer to fall **Hardiness:** hardy

I HAVE SEEN STOKES' ASTER GROW IN PARTIAL SHADE UNDER A walnut tree where nothing else would grow. This plant makes a great addition to a perennial cutting bed. The blue flowers combine well with coreopsis and other yellow flowering perennials—of course, I like blue and gold as they are the colors of my alma mater, the University of California. Stokes' Aster can be used in containers and combines well with low-growing summer annuals such as Lobelia or Sweet Alyssum.

Planting

Seeding: Direct sow or sow in flats in a cold frame in fall

Transplanting: Spring

Spacing: 15–18"

Growing

Stokes' Aster prefers to grow in **full sun** in **fertile, well-drained, moist, slightly acidic** soil. Ensure you supply adequate water. This plant can handle the heat, but winter protection should be provided where temperatures drop below 15° F. Divide in spring.

Tips

Stokes' Aster can be used in mixed or perennial borders or in beds. Extend the bloom time by immediately deadheading any spent flowers.

Contact with this plant may irritate skin allergies.

Recommended

S. laevis is a sturdy, upright, evergreen perennial with woolly, squarish stems. It grows 24" tall. '**Blue Danube**' grows 12–18" tall and bears large blue to lavender flowers.

Problems & Pests

May be affected by caterpillars or leaf spot.

With its decorative green bracts that arise from just underneath the flower, Stokes' Aster makes a good, long-lasting cut flower.

Stonecrop
Sedum

Height: 2–24" **Spread:** 12–24" or more **Flower color:** yellow, white, red, pink **Blooms:** summer, fall **Hardiness:** hardy to semi-hardy

STONECROPS ARE GREAT PLANTS FOR BEGINNING GARDENERS. These plants are forgiving when neglected, but respond equally well to tender loving care. They are favorites of gardeners who collect rock garden plants and unusual border plants. *S. acre* or 'Vera Jameson' can be used as groundcovers, while the cultivars 'Autumn Joy' or *S. spectabile* 'Brilliant' can be massed to provide beds of color. 'Autumn Joy' is increasing in popularity because it needs less water than many other perennials. Plant it with Roman Chamomile (*Chamaemelum nobile*), which will fill the space when 'Autumn Joy' is in its dormant state.

Planting

Seeding: Start seeds in containers in a cold frame in fall or indoors in early spring. Purchased seed is often a mix of different species. You might not get what you hoped for or expected, but you can just as easily be pleasantly surprised.

Transplanting: Spring

Spacing: 18"

Growing

Stonecrops prefer **full sun** but tolerate partial shade. The soil should be of **average fertility**, very **well drained** and **neutral to alkaline**. Though they are generally forgiving of neglect, they do not tolerate too much water or poor drainage. Divide in spring, when needed. Prune back 'Autumn Joy' in May by half and insert pruned-off parts into soft soil; cuttings will root quickly. Pruning upright species and hybrids in early summer will produce compact, bushy plants.

S. rubrotinctum (above), 'Autumn Joy' (below)

Low-growing stonecrops make excellent groundcovers under trees. Their shallow roots survive well in the competition for space and moisture.

S. spurium cultivar (above),
S. 'Vera Jameson' (below)

Species that produce young plants off a mother plant are easy to propagate by detaching and rooting the side shoots. Other stonecrop species, such as *S. spectabile*, are easily propagated from cuttings.

Tips

Low-growing stonecrops make excellent groundcovers and rock-garden or rock-wall plants. They also edge beds and borders wonderfully. The taller types give a beautiful display in a bed or border.

Recommended

S. acre (Gold Moss Stonecrop) grows 2" high and spreads indefinitely. The small, yellow-green flowers are borne from spring to early summer.

S. 'Autumn Joy' (Autumn Joy Sedum) is a popular upright hybrid. The flowers open pink or red and later fade to deep bronze over a long period in late summer and fall. The plant forms a clump 24" tall, with an equal spread. It should be cut back to the ground after the tops die back after blooming.

S. morganianum (Donkey Tail, Burro's Tail) is a succulent plant with light gray-green leaves on trailing stems growing 3–4' long over many years. Pale pink to deep red flowers are occasionally produced in spring to summer. The plants respond well to liquid organic fertilizer. Protect from wind and provide some afternoon shade.

S. rubrotinctum (Pork and Beans) is an evergreen, shrubby succulent plant with arching, branching, sometimes horizontal stems that root where they touch the ground. It grows 8–10" tall and 8" wide and bears star-shaped yellow flowers in winter and early spring. This plant is easily propagated by detaching and rooting the plump leaves.

S. spectabile (Showy Stonecrop) is an upright species with pink flowers borne in late summer. It forms a clump 18" tall and wide. **'Brilliant'** bears bright pink to deep rose-pink flowers.

S. spurium (Two-row Stonecrop) forms a mat about 4" tall and 24" wide. The summer flowers are deep pink or white.

S. **'Vera Jameson'** is a low, mounding plant with purple-tinged stems and pinkish-purple foliage. It grows up to 12" tall and spreads 18". Clusters of dark pink flowers are borne in late summer and fall.

Problems & Pests

Slugs, snails and scale insects may cause trouble for these plants.

S. spectabile cultivar (above), 'Brilliant' (below)

'Autumn Joy' brings color to the late-season garden, when few other flowers are in bloom.

Sweet Woodruff

Galium

Height: 12–18" **Spread:** indefinite **Flower color:** white **Blooms:** late spring to mid-summer **Hardiness:** hardy

SWEET WOODRUFF MAKES A GREAT GROUNDCOVER AROUND plantain lilies and other plants that go dormant in the winter. You can actually mow this groundcover if you set your lawnmower to cut to three inches high. Dispose of the cuttings in a plastic bag. Don't put the cuttings in your compost pile, or you will have lots and lots of Sweet Woodruff.

Planting

Seeding: Direct sow freshly ripe seed in fall

Transplanting: Spring; from flats

Spacing: 12"

Growing

Sweet Woodruff prefers **partial shade.** It will grow well, but will not bloom well, in full shade. The soil should be **humus rich, well drained** and **evenly moist.** Divide in early spring or fall. It will need feeding in summer, preferably with a liquid organic fertilizer.

Tips

Sweet Woodruff is a perfect wood-land groundcover. It loves the same conditions in which azaleas and rhododendrons thrive, and it forms a beautiful, aromatic, green carpet.

Sweet Woodruff self-seeds abundantly and may become invasive. Shear back after blooming to encourage plants to fill in with foliage and crowd out weeds.

Recommended

G. odoratum is a low, spreading groundcover producing clusters of star-shaped, white flowers.

Problems & Pests

Sweet Woodruff may have problems with mildew, rust and fungal leaf spot.

This plant is one of the ingredients of May Wine. A few springs of G. odoratum *are added to the mix one hour before serving.*

Thyme

Thymus

Height: 2–18" **Spread:** 4–36" **Flower color:** purple, pink, white
Blooms: late spring, summer **Hardiness:** hardy

ALL VARIETIES OF THYME HAVE A DISTINCTLY WONDERFUL
fragrance. The dried leaves are commonly used in cooking and are often
added to potpourri along with other fragrant foliage plants and roses.
Mother of Thyme *(T. serpyllum)* and Woolly Thyme *(T. pseudolanuginosus)*
make good groundcovers and are also useful in rock gardens. The blooms
of thyme plants attract bees, making them useful in vegetable gardens. All
thyme plants are totally deer proof and low water users.

Planting

Seeding: Many popular hybrids, particularly those with variegated leaves, cannot be grown from seed. Common Thyme and Mother of Thyme can be started from seed; start indoors in early spring.

Transplanting: Spring; from flats

Spacing: 4–36"

Growing

Thymes prefer **full sun** but benefit from afternoon shade in the hotter areas. The soil should be **average or poor** and very **well drained**; it helps to have leaf mold or peat moss worked in. Divide plants in spring.

It is easy to propagate the cultivars that cannot be started from seed. As the plants grow outwards, the branches touch the ground and send out new roots. These rooted stems may be removed and grown in pots to be transplanted the next spring. Unrooted stem cuttings may be taken in late spring to early summer, before flowering.

T. vulgaris (above), *T. serpyllum* (below)

This large genus has species around the world that were used in various ways in several cultures. Ancient Egyptians used thyme in embalming, the Greeks added it to baths, and the Romans purified their rooms with it.

T. serpyllum (above),
T. x citriodorus 'Argenteus' (below)

Tips

Thymes are useful plants to include in the front of borders, between or beside paving stones and on rock gardens and rock walls.

Once the plants have finished flowering, it is a good idea to shear them back by about half to encourage new growth and prevent the plants from becoming too woody. A lawnmower set at 2–3" will go a good job of cutting back. Make sure the mower blade is sharp.

Recommended

T. x citriodorus (Lemon-scented Thyme) forms a mound 12" tall and 18–24" wide. The foliage does smell of lemon, and the summer flowers are pale pink. The cultivars are more ornamental. '**Argenteus**' has silver-edged leaves. '**Aureus**' has yellow-gold variegated leaves. '**Golden King**' has yellow-margined leaves.

T. pseudolanuginosus (Woolly Thyme) is mat forming, reaching a height of only 2–3" and spreading 36". Pink flowers are produced sporadically in mid-summer and often not at all. This is the toughest of all of the thymes. It will tolerate drought once established.

T. serpyllum (Mother of Thyme, Wild Thyme) is a popular low-growing species. It usually grows 3–5" tall and spreads 24–36". The purple flowers bloom in summer. Many cultivars are available. '**Elfin**' forms tiny, dense mounds of foliage 2–3" tall and 4–5" wide. It rarely flowers. '**Minor**' grows 5" high with pink flowers. '**Snowdrift**' has white flowers.

T. vulgaris (Common Thyme) forms a bushy shrub of gray-green leaves. The late-spring to early-summer flowers may be purple, pink or white. It usually grows 12–18" tall and spreads 18–24". **'Argenteus'** has pale pink flowers and silver-edged leaves.

Problems & Pests

Thyme plants rarely have any problems. Seedlings may suffer from damping off and plants may get gray mold or root rot. Good circulation and adequate drainage help prevent these problems.

T. serpyllum is used today as a seasoning and in potpourris. T. vulgaris is the thyme usually used for commercially available seasoning.

T. serpyllum (above), 'Golden King' (below)

Torch Lily
Red-Hot Poker
Kniphofia

Height: 2–6' **Spread:** 18–24" **Flower color:** bright red, orange, pale yellow, cream white; the spikes appear bicolored when the buds and mature flowers are different colors **Blooms:** mid-summer to fall **Hardiness:** hardy

TORCH LILIES MAKE LONG-LASTING CUT flowers and add bold accents to any floral arrangement. They are great companion plants to many ornamental grasses and work very well planted under native oak trees. Only a modest amount of water or spot watering during the summer is necessary. On the Northern California coast, you will find these plants growing around old homes. They seem quite content without human intervention.

Planting

Seeding: Species may be started in containers in a cold frame in early spring; cultivars are unlikely to come true to type

Transplanting: On the coast, year-round; in the interior, January and February

Spacing: 18–24"

Torch lilies will attract hummingbirds and butterflies to your garden.

Growing

These plants grow equally well in **full sun** or **partial shade**. The soil should be **fertile, humus rich, sandy** and **moist**. Ensure adequate water when the plant is blooming. Large clumps may be divided in late spring, or in summer if the plant is flowering in spring. The plants perform best when left undivided for several years. The best method for propagating is to dig up off shoots of the mother plant without disturbing the main root system.

In areas where the temperature drops below 0° F, do not cut back the foliage in fall because it is needed for winter protection. Rather, bundle up the leaves and tie them above the center bud to keep the crown dry and protected. Ensure adequate drainage in winter. In warmer areas, simply remove any shabby growth in fall by pulling off unsightly leaves. Make sure you wear gloves when doing this: the edges of the leaves are serrated and tough.

Tips

Torch lilies make a bold, vertical statement in the middle or back of a border. They look best planted in groups.

To encourage the plants to continue flowering for as long as possible, cut the spent flowers off where the flower stem meets the plant.

Recommended

K. uvaria grows to a height of 3–4' with a spread of 18–24". Spikes of drooping bright red to orange-red flower buds open to yellow from

K. uvaria cultivars

late summer to early fall. '**Little Maid**' grows to only 24" tall and has salmon-colored buds opening to white flowers. '**Nobilis**' is a large plant growing up to 6' tall with long orange-red flower spikes, borne from mid-summer to fall.

Alternate Species

K. rooperi reaches a height of 4' and spreads 24". Red-orange buds open to yellow-orange from mid- to late summer.

Problems & Pests

Stem or crown rot and slugs and snails may cause problems. Thrips may cause flowers to drop off unopened. Mealybugs have been known to invade the crown.

Violet

Viola

Height: 3–8" **Spread:** 8–18" or more **Flower color:** shades of purple, blue, pink, white **Blooms:** late winter, spring, summer, sometimes again in fall **Hardiness:** hardy

MY GRANDMA PLANTED SWEET VIOLET UNDER AN OLD APPLE tree and picked the blooms for small fragrant bouquets that made the house smell especially nice. Sweet Violet is known for its fragrance. It makes a handsome addition to any perennial garden and is one of the best ground-covers for partial morning sun.

Planting

Seeding: Sow seed indoors in winter

Transplanting: Year-round; from six-packs and 4" pots

Spacing: 8–12"

Growing

Grow violets in **partial to full shade**. They tolerate some sunlight as long as shade from the hottest sun is provided. The soil should be **fertile, humus rich, moist** and **well drained**. Divide in spring or fall.

Violet species self-seed freely and you may find them cropping up in various places in the garden. Deadhead the flowers as they fade to extend the bloom and to reduce the amount of self-seeding. Most of the species listed also spread by runners. Cultivars may not set seed.

Tips

Violets are good for rock gardens, rock walls and the front of borders, but they can be invasive.

Add compost or planting mix around *V. adunca* and *V. odorata* to encourage spreading. *V. odorata* may become invasive.

V. sororia should be sheared back in fall and fertilized with compost or other organic material in spring to encourage healthy growth.

Recommended

V. adunca (California Sweet Violet, Western Dog Violet) is a compact plant growing only 3–6" tall and wide. It will continue to spread by runners and self-seeding. The fragrant flowers range in color from purple to blue and have orange stigmas and white at the petal bases.

V. odorata (Sweet Violet) is a sweet-scented plant that grows 8" tall and 12–18" wide. It will spread by runners and self-seeding. The flowers bloom from late winter to spring in deep violet, pinkish-blue or white. **'Queen Charlotte'** bears dark blue flowers on 6–8" tall plants. **'Rosina'** produces darker-centered pink flowers in abundance. **'Royal Robe'** grows to 6" tall and bears deep violet flowers in spring and again in fall.

V. sororia (Woolly Blue Violet) forms a small clump of foliage with fuzzy undersides. It grows 4" tall and spreads 8". Its flowers, borne in spring and summer, are purple or white with purple dots and streaks. *V. sororia* does not spread by runners but will self-seed prolifically. **'Freckles'** has white flowers that are speckled with light purple dots. It comes true to type from seed.

Problems & Pests

Slugs and snails may attack these plants. If Viola Midge is a problem, cut back blooms and spray the plants with horticultural oil.

Wallflower
Erysimum

Height: 12–36" **Spread:** 1–4' or more **Flower color:** yellow, orange, red, cream, bronze, burgundy, brown **Blooms:** Spring and fall in the interior valleys; all year in cool coastal areas **Hardiness:** hardy to semi-hardy

WITH ITS VIVID COLORS, ENGLISH WALLFLOWER IS A WONDERFUL addition to any garden. It is short-lived in most areas of Northern California but along the coast is considered a longer-living perennial. It will self-sow or you can collect the seeds and sow them yourself if you want more plants. They combine well with gray-foliage perennials such as sages, Lamb's Ears and *Lychnis coronaria*. 'Bowles' Mauve' should be replaced every three years from cuttings from the mother plant; otherwise, it will look woody and unattractive. Its gray-green foliage accents the wonderful lavender flowers. 'Compact Bowles Mauve' should also be replaced every two to three years. These short-lived plants just bloom themselves to death.

Planting

Seeding: Sow seeds in spring in flats in a cold frame. Seedlings may need to be transplanted a couple of times depending on their rate of growth.

Transplanting: Fall or early spring; available in most nurseries in bloom in spring

Spacing: 2–3'

Growing

Grow wallflower plants in **full sun** in **moist, well-drained, moderately fertile, neutral to alkaline** soil. Ensure you provide adequate water, especially with *E. cheiri*.

The plants can be lightly trimmed after flowering to promote more blooms and to keep the plant tidy. *E. cheiri* should be sheared back by one-third when it ends it original bloom cycle. It will bloom again after shearing. Propagate by seed or by softwood cuttings in summer.

Tips

Wallflower plants are great for beds or borders. They are also effective in rock gardens, on rock walls and in containers. The flowers of *E. cheiri* make good cut flowers.

Recommended

E. **'Bowles' Mauve'** is a roundish, evergreen, shrubby perennial growing 30–36" tall and spreading to 36" or more. Tall, spiky clusters of mauve flowers bloom almost continuously, especially where the winters are mild and the summers are cool. This plant can be short-lived. **'Compact Bowles Mauve'** grows 24" tall and wide.

E. cheiri

E. cheiri (English Wallflower) is an old favorite. It is an evergreen perennial that has upright, shrubby growth with a height of 12–30" and a spread of 12–18". Clusters of fragrant, orange-yellow flowers bloom in spring. Gardeners along the northern coast may get flowers all year long. The many cultivars come in shades of pink, red, orange, yellow, cream, burgundy, bronze and brown. **'Orange Bedder'** is part of the Bedder series. It grows to 12" tall and wide and produces many bright orange, fragrant flowers. Other cultivars in the Bedder series have flowers in shades of yellow, orange and red. This fragrant perennial will self-sow in all but the hottest areas in Northern California and makes a good cut flower.

Problems & Pests

Rust, white rust, powdery mildew, slugs, snails and caterpillars can cause problems. In some areas psyllids can make the foliage unattractive, but they do not harm the bloom cycle. If psyllids infect your plants, remove the plants and dispose of them in the garbage, not the compost pile.

Yarrow
Achillea

Height: 6–36" **Spread:** 12–24" **Flower color:** white, yellow, red, orange, pink **Blooms:** summer to early fall **Hardiness:** hardy

AS THE CALIFORNIA POPPIES AND NATIVE LUPINE FADE INTO FOND memories of spring, the native Yarrow comes forth, making a trip along California highways a joy. Because of our Mediterranean climate, they go dormant after blooming only to re-emerge after the fall rains. Yarrows are now available in a rainbow of colors, and all yarrows self-sow.

The native variety in California was used by the Native Americans as a tea for various ailments and was called 'life medicine.'

Planting

Seeding: Direct sow in spring. Don't cover the seeds; they need light to germinate.

Transplanting: Spring through early June; from one-gallon containers. It is best to pop these out of the container and divide at that time because they have been in those containers from the previous year.

Spacing: 12–24"

Growing

Grow yarrows in **full sun.** They prefer an **average to sandy** soil or any soil that is **well drained.** These plants will not do well in a heavy, wet soil, and they do not tolerate high humidity. They will, however, take a great deal of abuse, including drought and poor soil. Divide every four or five years, in spring or fall.

Remove the flowerheads once they begin to fade. Yarrows will flower more profusely and for longer periods if they are deadheaded.

Tips

Yarrows are very informal plants. They look best when grown in a natural-looking garden. Cottage gardens and wildflower gardens are perfect places to grow these plants. They thrive in hot, dry locations where nothing else will grow.

Yarrows make excellent groundcovers, even though they can be quite tall. The plants send up shoots and flowers from a low basal point and may be mowed periodically. The mower blades, however, should be kept quite high, no lower than 4".

'Cerise Queen' (above), 'Summer Pastels' (below)

Yarrow has blood-coagulating properties that were recognized by the ancient Greeks. Achillea *is named after the legendary Achilles because during the battle of Troy he treated the wounds of his warriors with this herb.*

Keep in mind that you are mowing off the flowerheads. Do not mow more often than once a month, or you will have short yarrow with no flowers!

Use yarrow flowers in fresh or dried arrangements. Pick the blooms only after pollen is visible on them, or they will die very quickly.

Recommended

A. ageratifolia (Greek Yarrow) forms mats of silvery foliage 6–10" tall and 12" wide. Clusters of tiny, white flowers are produced in summer.

A. millefolium (Common Yarrow) is 12–36" tall and up to 24" wide, bearing white flowers. The species is almost never grown in favor of the many cultivars that have been developed. The species and the cultivars spread by rhizomes and may become invasive. '**Cerise Queen**' has pinkish-red flowers. '**Fire King**' is a vigorous

A. millefolium cultivars (above),
A. millefolium (below)

grower that produces yellow-centered, red flowers. '**Salmon Beauty**' ('Lachsschönheit') bears salmon pink flowers. '**Summer Pastels**' has flowers of all colors. It is the most heat- and drought-tolerant cultivar, and it has fade-resistant flowers.

Problems & Pests

Watch for aphids. Yarrows may have occasional problems with rust, powdery mildew and stem rot. If fungal diseases occur, hold back on watering and cultivate around the plant to give it more air.

Druids used yarrow to divine the weather, and the early Chinese used it to foretell the future.

A. millefolium with *Phlox* and *Hemerocallis* (below)

Height Legend: Low: < 12" • Medium: 12–24" • Tall: > 24"

SPECIES by Common Name	COLOR								BLOOMING				HEIGHT		
	White	Pink	Red	Orange	Yellow	Blue	Purple	Foliage	Spring	Summer	Fall	Winter	Low	Medium	Tall
Anemone	*	*	*			*			*	*			*	*	*
Aster	*	*	*			*	*			*	*		*	*	*
Astilbe	*	*	*	*			*			*				*	*
Baby's Breath	*	*								*			*	*	*
Balloon Flower	*	*				*				*	*				*
Basket-of-Gold					*				*			*	*		
Bear's Breeches	*		*				*		*	*					*
Beard Tongue		*	*			*	*		*	*				*	*
Bee Balm		*	*							*					*
Bellflower	*	*				*	*		*	*			*	*	
Bergenia		*	*				*		*					*	
Bidens					*				*	*	*			*	*
Black-eyed Susan				*	*					*	*			*	*
Bleeding Heart	*	*								*	*			*	*
Blue Eyes						*			*	*				*	
Blue Marguerite						*				*			*	*	
Blue Star Flower						*			*	*				*	*
Butterfly Weed			*	*	*					*	*			*	*
California Poppy		*	*	*	*				*	*			*	*	
Candle Larkspur	*	*	*			*	*	*	*	*					*
Candytuft	*								*			*	*		
Cape Fuchsia		*	*	*						*	*			*	*
Cardinal Flower	*	*	*			*	*			*	*				*
Catmint	*	*				*	*		*	*				*	*
Columbine	*	*	*	*	*	*	*		*	*					*
Copper Canyon Daisy				*	*				*	*	*				*
Coral Bells	*	*	*				*		*	*				*	*
Coreopsis					*				*	*	*		*	*	*
Cranesbill	*	*	*			*	*		*	*	*		*	*	*
Dame's Rocket	*						*		*	*					*
Daylily		*	*	*	*		*		*	*				*	*

HARDINESS			LIGHT				IDEAL SOIL CONDITIONS						Page Number	SPECIES by Common Name
Hardy	Semi-hardy	Tender	Sun	Partial Shade	Light Shade	Shade	Moist	Well Drained	Dry	Fertile	Average	Poor		
*	*			*	*		*	*		*	*		70	Anemone
*	*		*	*			*	*		*			74	Aster
*				*	*	*	*	*		*			78	Astilbe
*			*					*			*		82	Baby's Breath
*			*	*			*	*		*	*		86	Balloon Flower
*			*	*	*			*			*	*	88	Basket-of-Gold
*			*	*	*	*		*					90	Bear's Breeches
*			*	*				*		*	*	*	94	Beard Tongue
*			*	*			*	*			*		98	Bee Balm
*			*	*	*			*		*	*		102	Bellflower
*				*	*	*	*	*		*	*		106	Bergenia
	*		*				*	*		*	*		110	Bidens
*			*	*				*			*		112	Black-eyed Susan
*				*	*	*	*	*		*	*		114	Bleeding Heart
*				*	*		*	*		*	*		118	Blue Eyes
	*		*					*			*		120	Blue Marguerite
*				*			*	*		*	*		122	Blue Star Flower
*			*					*			*	*	124	Butterfly Weed
*			*					*			*	*	126	California Poppy
*			*				*	*		*			130	Candle Larkspur
*			*				*	*			*	*	134	Candytuft
	*		*		*		*	*		*			136	Cape Fuchsia
*	*		*	*			*			*			138	Cardinal Flower
*			*	*				*			*		142	Catmint
*			*	*			*	*		*			146	Columbine
	*		*					*		*			150	Copper Canyon Daisy
*				*	*		*	*		*	*		152	Coral Bells
*	*		*					*			*		156	Coreopsis
*				*	*	*		*			*		160	Cranesbill
*			*	*			*	*		*	*		164	Dame's Rocket
*			*	*	*	*	*	*		*			166	Daylily

Height Legend: Low: < 12" • Medium: 12–24" • Tall: > 24"

SPECIES by Common Name	COLOR								BLOOMING				HEIGHT		
	White	Pink	Red	Orange	Yellow	Blue	Purple	Foliage	Spring	Summer	Fall	Winter	Low	Medium	Tall
Dianthus	*	*	*						*	*			*	*	
Dusty Miller					*			*		*			*	*	*
Euphorbia					*				*			*		*	*
Evening Primrose	*	*							*	*	*		*		
False Rockcress						*	*		*				*		
Fan Flower						*	*		*	*	*	*	*	*	*
Fleabane	*	*					*			*				*	
Foamflower	*	*							*					*	
Foxglove	*	*							*		*				*
Gaura	*	*							*	*					*
Gayfeather	*						*			*					*
Geranium	*	*	*	*			*		*	*	*		*	*	*
Geum			*	*	*				*	*				*	
Globe Thistle						*				*	*		*	*	*
Golden Marguerite				*	*					*	*				*
Gunnera			*							*					*
Hellebore	*	*					*		*			*		*	
Hens and Chicks		*	*				*			*			*		
Hibiscus	*	*	*							*	*			*	*
Himalayan Poppy				*	*	*	*		*	*	*			*	*
Iris	*	*	*		*	*	*		*	*			*	*	*
Jacob's Ladder	*					*	*		*	*			*	*	*
Lady's Mantle					*					*	*		*	*	
Lamb's Ears		*					*		*	*			*	*	
Lantana	*	*	*	*			*		*	*				*	*
Lavender Cotton					*			*		*				*	*
Ligularia				*	*					*	*				*
Lily-of-the-Nile						*	*			*				*	*
Lion's Tail			*	*						*	*				*
Lithodora						*			*	*			*		
Lungwort	*	*	*			*	*		*			*	*	*	

Hardy	Semi-hardy	Tender	Sun	Partial Shade	Light Shade	Shade	Moist	Well Drained	Dry	Fertile	Average	Poor	Page Number	SPECIES by Common Name
*			*				*	*			*		170	Dianthus
*	*		*					*			*		174	Dusty Miller
*			*				*	*			*		176	Euphorbia
*			*								*	*	180	Evening Primrose
*			*				*	*			*		182	False Rockcress
	*		*				*	*			*		184	Fan Flower
*	*		*		*			*		*	*		186	Fleabane
*				*	*	*	*						188	Foamflower
*				*	*	*	*			*			190	Foxglove
*			*					*		*			194	Gaura
*			*				*	*			*		196	Gayfeather
	*		*					*		*			198	Geranium
*			*				*	*		*			204	Geum
*			*					*			*	*	206	Globe Thistle
*			*					*			*		208	Golden Marguerite
	*		*	*			*			*			210	Gunnera
*					*	*	*	*		*			212	Hellebore
*			*	*							*	*	214	Hens and Chicks
*			*				*	*			*		218	Hibiscus
*	*			*	*	*	*	*			*		222	Himalayan Poppy
*	*		*					*		*	*		224	Iris
*				*	*	*	*	*		*			228	Jacob's Ladder
*				*	*		*	*		*			230	Lady's Mantle
*			*					*			*	*	232	Lamb's Ears
	*	*	*				*	*			*		234	Lantana
*			*					*			*	*	238	Lavender Cotton
*				*	*	*	*			*			240	Ligularia
*				*	*	*	*	*		*			242	Lily-of-the-Nile
	*		*					*		*	*		246	Lion's Tail
*			*					*					248	Lithodora
*				*	*	*	*	*		*			250	Lungwort

Height Legend: Low: < 12" • Medium: 12–24" • Tall: > 24"

SPECIES by Common Name	White	Pink	Red	Orange	Yellow	Blue	Purple	Foliage	Spring	Summer	Fall	Winter	Low	Medium	Tall
Lupine	*	*	*		*	*				*				*	*
Mallow	*	*				*	*			*	*		*	*	*
Marsh Marigold	*				*				*				*	*	
Meadow Rue	*	*			*		*		*	*					*
Meadowsweet	*	*								*					*
Monkey Flower		*	*	*	*				*	*			*	*	*
Monkshood	*					*	*			*					*
Obedient Plant	*	*				*	*			*	*			*	*
Oriental Poppy	*	*	*				*		*	*				*	*
Peony	*	*	*		*		*		*	*				*	*
Peruvian Lily		*	*	*	*				*	*					*
Phlox	*	*	*				*		*	*			*	*	*
Pincushion Flower	*	*				*	*		*	*	*			*	*
Plantain Lily	*						*	*		*	*		*	*	*
Purple Coneflower	*						*		*	*				*	*
Rock Cress	*	*					*		*				*		
Russian Sage						*			*	*					*
Salvia	*	*	*			*	*		*	*	*			*	*
Sandwort	*								*	*			*		
Sea Holly	*					*	*			*				*	*
Sea Pink	*	*	*						*	*			*	*	
Shasta Daisy	*									*	*				*
Soapwort	*	*	*						*	*			*	*	
Stokes' Aster	*					*	*			*	*			*	
Stonecrop	*	*	*		*					*	*		*	*	
Sweet Woodruff	*								*	*				*	
Thyme	*	*					*		*	*			*	*	
Torch Lily	*		*	*	*					*	*				*
Violet	*	*				*	*		*	*		*	*		
Wallflower		*		*	*		*		*	*	*	*		*	*
Yarrow	*	*	*	*	*					*	*		*	*	*

HARDINESS			LIGHT				IDEAL SOIL CONDITIONS						Page Number	SPECIES by Common Name
Hardy	Semi-hardy	Tender	Sun	Partial Shade	Light Shade	Shade	Moist	Well Drained	Dry	Fertile	Average	Poor		
*			*				*	*		*	*		252	Lupine
*			*				*	*			*		256	Mallow
*				*	*		*						260	Marsh Marigold
*				*	*		*	*			*		262	Meadow Rue
*			*	*	*	*	*		*	*			266	Meadowsweet
*				*	*	*	*			*			270	Monkey Flower
*			*		*		*			*			272	Monkshood
*			*				*				*		276	Obedient Plant
*			*					*			*		278	Oriental Poppy
*			*	*			*	*		*			282	Peony
*	*		*	*			*	*			*		286	Peruvian Lily
*	*		*	*			*	*		*			288	Phlox
*			*	*				*			*		292	Pincushion Flower
*				*	*	*	*	*		*			294	Plantain Lily
*			*		*					*	*		298	Purple Coneflower
*	*		*					*			*	*	302	Rock Cress
*			*					*			*	*	304	Russian Sage
*	*		*				*	*		*	*		306	Salvia
*			*		*		*	*			*		310	Sandwort
*			*					*			*	*	312	Sea Holly
*			*					*			*	*	314	Sea Pink
*			*				*	*		*			316	Shasta Daisy
*			*				*	*			*		318	Soapwort
*			*				*	*		*			320	Stokes' Aster
*	*		*					*			*		322	Stonecrop
*				*			*	*			*		326	Sweet Woodruff
*			*					*			*	*	328	Thyme
*			*	*			*	*		*			332	Torch Lily
*				*	*	*	*	*		*			334	Violet
*	*		*				*	*			*		336	Wallflower
*			*					*			*		338	Yarrow

Glossary of Terms

acid soil: soil with a pH lower than 7.0

alkaline soil: soil with a pH higher than 7.0

annual: a plant that germinates, flowers, sets seed and dies in one growing season

basal leaves: leaves that form from the crown

biennial: a plant that germinates and produces stems, roots and leaves in the first growing season; it flowers, sets seed and dies in the second growing season

crown: the part of a plant at or just below soil level where the shoots join the roots

cultivar: a cultivated plant variety with one or more distinct differences from the species, such as flower color, leaf variegation or disease resistance

damping off: fungal disease causing seedlings to rot at soil level and topple over

deadhead: to remove spent flowers to maintain a neat appearance and encourage a longer blooming period

desiccation: drying out of plant tissue, especially foliage

disbud: to remove some flower buds to improve the size or quality of those remaining

dormancy: a period of plant inactivity, usually during winter or unfavorable climatic conditions

double flower: a flower with an unusually large number of petals, often caused by mutation of the stamens into petals

forma (f.): a naturally occurring variant of a species; below the level of subspecies in biological classification; similar to variety

genus: a category of biological classification between the species and family levels; the first word in a Latin name indicates the genus

harden off: to gradually acclimatize plants that have been growing in a protective environment to a more harsh environment, e.g., plants started indoors being moved outdoors

hardy: capable of surviving unfavorable conditions, such as cold weather

humus: decomposed or decomposing organic material in the soil

hybrid: a plant resulting from natural or human-induced crossbreeding between varieties, species, or genera; the hybrid expresses features of each parent plant

neutral soil: soil with a pH of 7.0

node: the area on a stem from which a leaf or new shoot grows

pH: a measure of acidity or alkalinity (the lower the pH, the higher the acidity); the pH of soil influences availability of nutrients for plants

perennial: a plant that takes three or more years to complete its life cycle; a herbaceous perennial normally dies back to the ground over winter

quilled: refers to the narrow, tubular shape of petals or florets of certain flowers

rhizome: a food-storing stem that grows horizontally at or just below soil level, from which new shoots may emerge

rootball: the root mass and surrounding soil of a container-grown plant or a plant dug out of the ground

runner: a modified stem that grows on the soil surface; roots and new shoots are produced at nodes along its length

semi-double flower: a flower with petals that form two or three rings

semi-hardy: a plant capable of surviving the climatic conditions of a given region if protected

side-dressing: applying fertilizer to the soil beside or around a plant during the growing season to stimulate growth

single flower: a flower with a single ring of typically four or five petals

species: the original species from which cultivars and varieties are derived; the fundamental unit of biological classification

subspecies (subsp.): a naturally occurring, regional form of a species, often isolated from other subspecies but still potentially interfertile with them

taproot: a root system consisting of one main root with smaller roots branching from it

tender: incapable of surviving the climatic conditions of a given region and requiring protection from frost or cold

tepal: a sepal or petal of a flower, when the petals and sepals are not clearly distinguished from each other

true: the passing of desirable characteristics from the parent plant to seed-grown offspring; also called breeding true to type

tuber: the thick section of a rhizome bearing nodes and buds

variegation: foliage that has more than one color, often patched or striped or bearing differently colored leaf margins

variety (var.): a naturally occurring variant of a species; below the level of subspecies in biological classification

Glossary of Pests & Diseases

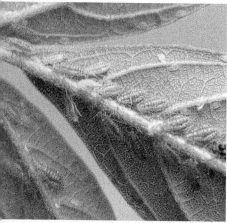

Caterpillar eating flowers

Aphids (center), Ladybird beetle larva (below)

Anthracnose

Fungus. Yellow or brown spots on leaves; sunken lesions and blisters on stems; can kill plant.
What to Do. Choose resistant varieties and cultivars; keep soil well drained; thin out stems to improve air circulation; avoid handling wet foliage. Remove and destroy infected plant parts; clean up and destroy debris from infected plants at end of growing season. Liquid copper spray can prevent the spread of the disease to other susceptible plants.

Ants

Most ants are beneficial in that they eat decomposing material, which adds to the cultivation of the soil. But they can also carry damaging, sucking insects such as whiteflies and aphids to other plants. The ants use the sucking insects' excrement (honeydew) as food for their colony. To control the sucking insects, you must eliminate ants.
What to Do. Eliminate ants with a solution of boric acid, sugar and water. See recipe on page 67.

Aphids

Tiny, pear-shaped insects, winged or wingless; green, black, brown, red or gray. Cluster along stems, on buds and on leaves. Suck sap from plants; cause distorted or stunted growth. Sticky honeydew forms on surfaces and encourages sooty mold growth.
What to Do. Squish small colonies by hand; dislodge them with water spray; spray serious infestations with insecticidal soap or horticultural oil; many predatory insects and birds feed on them.

Aster Yellows

Virus transmitted by insects called leafhoppers. Causes stunted or deformed growth; leaves become yellowed and deformed, flowers dwarfed and greenish; can kill plant.

What to Do. Control leafhoppers with insecticidal soap; remove and destroy infected plants; destroy any local weeds sharing the symptoms. Plant resistant varieties.

Beetles

Many types and sizes; usually rounded in shape with hard, shell-like outer wings covering membranous inner wings. Some are beneficial, e.g., ladybird beetles ('ladybugs'); others, e.g., June beetles, eat plants. Larvae: see Borers, Grubs. Leave wide range of chewing damage: make small or large holes in or around margins of leaves; consume entire leaves or areas between leaf veins ('skeletonize'); may also chew holes in flowers.

What to Do. Pick beetles off at night and drop them into an old coffee can half filled with soapy water (soap prevents them from floating); spread an old sheet under plants and shake off beetles to collect and dispose of them. Use a hand-held vacuum cleaner to remove them from the plant. Beneficial nematodes are effective control if the beetle goes through a part of its growing cycle in the ground.

Borers

Larvae of some moths, wasps, beetles; among the most damaging plant pests. Burrow into plant stems, branches, leaves and/or roots; destroy vascular tissue (plant veins and arteries) and structural strength. Worm-like; vary in size and get bigger as they bore through plants. Burrow and weaken stems to cause breakage; leaves will wilt; may see tunnels in leaves, stems or roots; rhizomes may be hollowed out entirely or in part.

What to Do. May be able to squish borers within leaves. Remove and destroy bored parts; may need to dig up and destroy infected roots and rhizomes.

Budworms (Geranium Budworm, Tobacco Budworm)

Moth larvae. $1/2$ to $3/4$" long; striped; green, yellow-green, tan, dull red; bore

Lygus Bug enjoying annual cosmos

into buds, eat from inside out and sometimes on open flowers; also eat new leaf growth; buds and new leaves appear tattered or ridden with holes.

What to Do. Pick off by hand daily and drop in soapy water. Remove infested plants and destroy. Apply preventative spray of B.t. (Bacillus thuringiensis) on mature plants. Do not re-plant susceptible varieties.

Bugs (True Bugs)

Small insects, up to $1/2$" long; green, brown, black or brightly colored and patterned. Many beneficial; a few pierce plants to suck out sap. Toxins may be injected that deform plants; sunken areas left where pierced; leaves rip as they grow; leaves, buds and new growth may be dwarfed and deformed.

What to Do. Remove debris and weeds from around plants in fall to destroy overwintering sites. Pick off by hand and drop into soapy water. Use parasitic nematodes if part of the bug's growth cycle is in the ground.

Caterpillars

Larvae of butterflies, moths, sawflies. Include budworms (see Budworms), cutworms (see Cutworms), leaf rollers, leaf tiers, loopers. Chew foliage and

Moth on strawflower

buds. Can completely defoliate a plant if infestation severe.
What to Do. Removal from plant is best control. Use high-pressure water and soap, or pick caterpillars off by hand. Control biologically using the naturally occurring soil bacterium *Bacillus thuringiensis* var. *kurstaki*, or *B.t.* for short (commercially available), which breaks down gut lining of caterpillars.

Cutworms

Larvae of some moths. About 1" long; plump, smooth-skinned caterpillars; curl up when poked or disturbed. Usually affect only young plants and seedlings, which may be completely chewed off at ground level.
What to Do. Pick off by hand. Create physical barriers from old toilet tissue rolls to make collars around plant bases; push tubes at least halfway into ground. Another trick is to put three toothpicks around each plant; make sure the toothpicks are right up against the stem.

Earwigs

Beneficial to a certain point when their population is low. In great numbers they eat plant materials, including flower buds, leaves and roots. They normally do not kill a plant, but make it unsightly.
What to Do. Roll up wet newspaper and place it in the garden at night. Earwigs will crawl in to the dark, wet paper. In the morning unroll newspaper and dump earwigs into a solution of soapy water. In a few weeks the population will be reduced.

Gray Mold (Botrytis Blight)

Fungal disease. Leaves, stems and flowers blacken, rot and die.
What to Do. Thin stems to improve air circulation, keep mulch away from base of plant, particularly in spring when plant starts to sprout; remove debris from garden at end of growing season; do not overwater. Remove and destroy any infected plant parts. Use horticultural oil as a preventative measure. Compost tea is also effective.

Grubs

Larvae of different beetles, commonly found below soil level; usually curled in C-shape. Body white or gray; head may be white, gray, brown or reddish. Problematic in lawns; may feed on plant roots. Plant wilts despite regular watering; may pull easily out of ground in severe cases.
What to Do. Toss any grubs found while digging onto a stone path or patio for birds to devour; apply parasitic nematodes or milky disease spore to infested soil (ask at your local garden center).

Leaf Miners

Tiny, stubby larvae of some butterflies and moths; may be yellow or green. Tunnel within leaves leaving winding trails; tunneled areas lighter in color than rest of leaf. Unsightly rather than health risk to plant.

Leaf miner damage

What to Do. Remove debris from area in fall to destroy overwintering sites; attract parasitic wasps with nectar plants such as yarrows. Remove and destroy infected foliage; can sometimes squish by hand within leaf. Floating row covers prevent eggs from being laid on plant. Bright blue sticky cards, available in most nurseries and through mail order, will attract and trap adult leaf miners.

Leaf Spot

Two common types: one caused by bacteria and the other by fungi. *Bacterial:* small speckled spots grow to encompass entire leaves; brown or purple in color; leaves may drop. *Fungal:* black, brown or yellow spots; leaves wither.
What to Do. Bacterial infection more severe; must remove entire plant. For fungal infection, remove and destroy infected plant parts. Sterilize removal tools; avoid wetting foliage or touching wet foliage; remove and destroy debris at end of growing season. Spray plant with liquid copper. Compost tea also works in most instances.

Mealybugs

Tiny crawling insects related to aphids; appear to be covered with white fuzz or flour. Sucking damage stunts and stresses plant. Mealybugs excrete honeydew, which promotes growth of sooty mold.
What to Do. Remove by hand on smaller plants; wash plant off with soap and water; wipe off with alcohol-soaked swabs; remove leaves with heavy infestations; encourage or introduce natural predators such as mealybug destroyer beetle and parasitic wasps; spray with insecticidal soap. Keep in mind larvae of mealybug destroyer beetles look like very large mealybugs. Always check plants for mealybugs before buying.

Mildew

Two types, both caused by fungus, but with slightly different symptoms. *Downy mildew:* yellow spots on upper sides of leaves and downy fuzz on undersides; fuzz may be yellow, white

Powdery mildew on zinnia

or gray. *Powdery mildew:* white or gray powdery coating on leaf surfaces that doesn't brush off.
What to Do. Choose resistant cultivars; space plants well; thin stems to encourage air circulation; tidy any debris in fall. Remove and destroy infected leaves or other parts. Spray compost tea or highly diluted fish emulsion (1 teaspoon per quart of water) to control powdery mildew. Control downy mildew by spraying foliage with a mixture of 5 tablespoons of horticultural oil and 2 teaspoons of baking soda per gallon of water. Three applications at one-week intervals will be needed.

Nematodes

Tiny worms that give plants disease symptoms. One type infects foliage and stems; the other infects roots. *Foliar:* yellow spots that turn brown on leaves; leaves shrivel and wither; problem starts on lowest leaves and works up plant. *Root-knot:* plant is stunted; may wilt; yellow spots on leaves; roots have tiny bumps or knots.
What to Do. Mulch soil, add organic matter, clean up debris in fall. Don't touch wet foliage of infected plants; can add parasitic nematodes to soil. Remove infected plants in extreme cases.

Snail eating leaf

Psyllids

Tiny, gnat-like insects that suck juice out of plant leaves, causing foliage to yellow, curl and die or appear brown and blasted; may leave sticky honeydew on leaves, encouraging sooty mold growth. Adults are $^1/_{10}$" long, green or brown and have wings; young nymphs have a white, waxy coating and are nearly immobile.
What to Do. Remove and destroy infested plants; do not put infested plants in compost bin. Keep area free of weeds. Ensure good fall clean up. Diatomaceous earth (not the kind used for swimming pools) or sulfur dusted on foliage may kill nymphs.

Rot

Several different fungi that affect different parts of the plant and can kill plant. *Crown rot:* affects base of plant, causing stems to blacken and fall over and leaves to yellow and wilt. *Root rot:* leaves yellow and plant wilts; digging up plant will show roots rotted away.
What to Do. Keep soil well drained; don't damage plant if you are digging around it; keep mulches away from plant base. Remove any infected plants.

Rust

Fungi. Pale spots on upper leaf surfaces; orange, fuzzy or dusty spots on leaf undersides.
What to Do. Choose rust-resistant varieties and cultivars; avoid handling wet leaves; ensure good air circulation;

use horticultural oil to protect new foliage; clean up garden debris at end of season. Remove and destroy infected plant parts. Do not put infected plants in compost pile.

Slugs & Snails

Slugs lack shells; snails have a spiral shell; both have slimy, smooth skin; can be up to 8" long; gray, green, black, beige, yellow or spotted. Leave large ragged hole in leaves and silvery slime trails on and around plants.
What to Do. Attach strips of copper to wood around raised beds or smaller boards inserted around susceptible groups of plants; slugs and snails will get shocked if they touch copper surfaces. Pick off by hand in the evening and squish with boot or drop in can of soapy water. Spread wood ash, oyster shells or diatomaceous earth (available in garden centers) on ground around plants; it will pierce their soft bodies and cause them to dehydrate. (CAUTION: do not use the diatomaceous earth that is used for swimming pool filters.) Use slug and snail bait, also available at local garden centers. Beer in a shallow dish may be effective.

Smut

Fungus. Attacks any above-ground plant parts including leaves, stems and flowers. Forms fleshy white galls that turn black and powdery.
What to Do. Remove and destroy infected plants. Avoid planting same plants in that spot for next few years.

Sooty Mold

Fungus. Thin black film forms on leaf surfaces and reduces amount of light getting to leaf surfaces.
What to Do. Wipe mold off leaf surfaces; control insects such as aphids, mealybugs and whiteflies (honeydew left on leaves encourages mold).

Spider Mites

Almost invisible to the naked eye; relatives of spiders without their insect-eating habits. Tiny; eight-legged; may spin webs; red, yellow or green; usually found on undersides of plant leaves. Suck juice out of leaves; may see fine webbing on leaves and stems; may see mites moving on leaf undersides; leaves become discolored and speckled in appearance, then turn brown and shrivel up.

What to Do. Wash off with a strong spray of water daily until all signs of infestation are gone; predatory mites are available through garden centers; spray plants with insecticidal soap. Apply horticultural oil.

Thrips

Difficult to see; may be visible if you disturb them by blowing gently on an infested flower. Yellow, black or brown; tiny, slender; narrow fringed wings. Suck juice out of plant cells, particularly in flowers and buds, causing gray mottled petals and leaves, dying buds and distorted and stunted growth.

What to Do. Remove and destroy infected plant parts; encourage native predatory insects with nectar plants such as yarrows; spray severe infestations with insecticidal soap. Use horticultural oil at 5 tablespoons per gallon. Use sticky blue cards to attract and trap adults.

Viruses

Plant may be stunted and leaves and flowers distorted, streaked or discolored. Viral diseases in plants cannot be controlled.

What to Do. Destroy infected plants; control insects such as aphids, leafhoppers and whiteflies that spread disease.

Whiteflies

Tiny flying insects that flutter up into the air when the plant is disturbed. Tiny; moth-like; white; live on undersides of plant leaves. Suck juice out of plant leaves, causing yellowed leaves and weakened plants; leave sticky honeydew on leaves, encouraging sooty mold growth.

What to Do. Destroy weeds where insects may live. Attract native predatory beetles and parasitic wasps with nectar plants such as yarrows; spray severe cases with insecticidal soap. Can make a sticky flypaper-like trap by mounting tin can on stake; wrap can with yellow paper and cover with clear baggie smeared with petroleum jelly; replace baggie when full of flies. Yellow sticky cards are also available from local nurseries and garden centers. Plant Sweet Alyssum in the immediate area. Make a spray by boiling old coffee grounds (see recipe p. 66) and use liquid as a spray.

Wilt

If watering hasn't helped a wilted plant, one of two wilt fungi may be at fault. *Fusarium wilt:* plant wilts, leaves turn yellow then die; symptoms generally appear first on one part of plant before spreading to other parts. *Verticillium wilt:* plant wilts; leaves curl up at edges; leaves turn yellow then drop off; plant may die.

What to Do. Both wilts difficult to control. Choose resistant plant varieties and cultivars; clean up debris at end of growing season. Destroy infected plants; solarize (sterilize) soil before re-planting—contact local garden center for assistance.

Ladybird beetles are beneficial garden predators.

Index

Page numbers in **bold** indicate main flower headings.